Maths mastery with greater depth

Year 3

Caroline Clissold

Introduction

What is mastery?

'Mastery' is a word that has become a key focus of teaching over the last couple of years.

The essential idea behind mastery is that all pupils need a deep understanding of the mathematics they are learning to ensure that future mathematical learning is built on solid foundations.

According to the National Centre for Excellence in the Teaching of Mathematics (NCETM), mastery is 'the development of deep structural knowledge and the ability to make connections. Making connections in mathematics deepens knowledge of concepts and procedures, ensures what is learnt is sustained over time, and cuts down the time required to assimilate and master later concepts and techniques.'

What is mastery with greater depth?

Developing mastery with greater depth is characterised by pupils' ability to solve problems with greater complexity (where the approach is not immediately obvious), demonstrating an imaginative and creative handling. Pupils working at greater depth can communicate results clearly and explain their understanding to others.

How to use this book

This book includes a set of sophisticated mathematical problems for each National Curriculum requirement. The 80 challenge questions included in the book can be adapted and varied to suit most pupils. Variation is an important factor of mastery. Variation is the art of sequencing similar but increasingly complex problems with the aim of pupils spotting patterns and understanding the underlying structure of the mathematics.

Applying variation to the tasks in this book will mean you can easily extend the problems that you give to pupils. Suitable variations are described in the challenge answers and notes, where appropriate. Ask pupils what they notice about the variation, what is happening and why.

Detailed answers to all challenges, plus assessment guidance and notes, will help you to assess whether pupils are achieving mastery with greater depth. The guidance includes information about what evidence of mastery you might see and suggests questions you could ask to uncover pupils' thinking. It also includes details of what to check and what that tells you, questioning in order to prompt or check reasoning and other things to be aware of.

Contents

Acknowledgements

Published by Keen Kite Books
An imprint of HarperCollins*Publishers* Ltd
1 London Bridge Street
London
SE1 9GF

Images and Illustrations are © Shutterstock.com and © HarperCollins*Publishers* Ltd

Text and design © 2017 Keen Kite Books, an imprint of HarperCollins*Publishers* Ltd

10 9 8 7 6 5 4 3 2 1

ISBN 9780008244675

The author asserts their moral right to be identified as the author of this work.

British Library Cataloguing in Publication Data
A catalogue record for this publication is available from the British Library.

Author: Caroline Clissold
Commissioning Editor: Michelle I'Anson and Shelley Teasdale
Project Management: Fiona Watson
Editor: Caroline Petherick
Cover Design: Anthony Godber
Internal design and illustrations: QBS Learning
Production: Natalia Rebow

Number – Number and place value

Counting

Challenge 1: Fahmida is counting in 4s and 8s.

Is she correct?

Explain your thinking to a friend.

When you have done that, write your explanation on paper.

> I think all the numbers that I say when I count in 4s and 8s will be even.

Challenge 2: Tom is counting in 50s and 100s.

Is he correct?

Explain your thinking to a friend.

When you have done that, write your explanation on paper.

> I think counting in 50s to 1000 would take half the counts that it would take if counting in 100s.

Place value

Challenge 3: Write all the three-digit numbers you can make using these digits.

| 9 | 7 | 4 | 5 |

How do you know you have them all?

Prove it to your friend.

Now, write your explanation on paper.

Which is the greatest number? Which is the least?

Can you make the number which is closest to 500? Prove it.

Challenge 4:

> I made a three-digit number that is more than 800 and less than 900, using these digits.
>
> | 8 | 7 | 9 | 6 |

What numbers could Fahmida have made? Find all the possibilities. Make a list of them.

How do you know you have them all?

Write an explanation to show what you did.

Challenge 1 Answer

Fahmida is correct; 4 and 8 are both multiples of two. Multiples of two are all even, so counting in multiples of two will always give even numbers.

Assessment

During the task, notice if the pupils work systematically, listing the counts in order. If they don't, systematic working is something they may need to focus on.

Once they have proved Fahmida is correct, assess their confidence in explaining in writing their reasoning as to why she is correct. Doing this independently and accurately would indicate depth of mastery.

Ask the pupils to list the numbers if Fahmida counted in steps of 6. Are these all even numbers as well?

Note

Ensure that pupils know the meaning of 'multiple'. Knowing the correct vocabulary will make explanations simpler and more succinct.

Encourage pupils to use what they know, and count in steps of 40, 80, 400, 800 and so on. In Year 3 they count in tenths. Can they apply this, and count in steps of $\frac{4}{10}$ and $\frac{8}{10}$? As they count, find out if they can reason, for example, that if they know $\frac{10}{10}$ is one whole then $\frac{16}{10}$ is equivalent to 1 and $\frac{6}{10}$.

If any pupils are not fluent at recalling their multiplication facts for 4 and 8, it would be important to practise these.

Challenge 2 Answer

Tom is incorrect. It will take him 20 counts to count to 1000 in 50s, but only 10 counts to count to 1000 in 100s.

Assessment

Do the pupils prove that Tom is incorrect by systematically listing the multiples of 50 and 100 to find out how many counts there are?

Ask the pupils to think of a reason why Tom thought that there would be half as many counts to count in 50s to 1000. He might have thought that because 50 is half of 100 there would have been half as many counts – but Tom needs to see that there are twice as many numbers when counting in multiples of 50 compared to multiples of 100.

What can the pupils tell you about counting in 50s and 100s? Do they recognise that 50 and 100 are multiples of 2, 5 and 10?

Note

Ensure that pupils know the meaning of 'multiple'. Knowing the correct vocabulary will make explanations simpler and more succinct.

Encourage pupils to use what they know; for example that there are two 50s in 100, so there are four 50s in 200, six in 300 and so on.

In Year 3 they count in tenths. Can they apply their knowledge of counting in 50s and 100s to count in steps of five-tenths, tenths and hundredths? It would be a good idea to teach this area of the fractions requirements in counting and place value. As pupils count, stop them and find out if they can reason that, for example, if they know $\frac{10}{10}$ is one whole, then $\frac{50}{50}$ is one whole so $\frac{100}{50}$ must be two wholes.

National Curriculum objective, Year 3, Number and place value

- *recognise the place value of each digit in a three-digit number (hundreds, tens, ones)*
- *find 10 or 100 more or less than a given number*

Challenge 3 Answer

974, 947, 975, 957, 945, 954, 794, 749, 795, 759, 745, 754, 497, 479, 475, 457, 495, 459, 597, 579, 594, 549, 574, 547

Greatest number: 975

Least number: 457

Closest to 500: 497

Assessment

During the task, notice if the pupils work systematically, listing the numbers as in the answer section or in a similar systematic way. If they don't, systematic working is something they may need to focus on. Are they showing perseverance and resilience, a determination to find all possibilities? Can they find them?

Identifying the greatest and least numbers is simple. When finding the number closest to 500, pupils often think that a number with 5 in the hundreds position will be closest. Can they identify that 497 is only three away from 500 and that the lowest number with 5 in the hundreds is 47 higher than 500?

Assess how they prove that they have found all the numbers. Look out for pupils who write that they began with 9 in the 100s and then put another digit in the tens and a third in the ones, then swapped the last two digits over. They repeat this explanation for the other digits in the 100s position. If they can do both these things independently, they are working with a greater depth of mastery. If they can't, make one of these areas something to focus on with the class.

Challenge 4 Answer

879, 897, 876, 867, 896, 869

Assessment

Watch the pupils work through the task. Do they realise that they don't need to find numbers that have 6, 7 and 9 in the hundreds position, because these will be either greater than or less than numbers between 800 and 900?

As they work are they showing a systematic approach?

You could ask pupils to list the numbers that are 10 more and 10 less than those they have made. You could also ask them to list the numbers that are 100 more and 100 less. When they add 10 to 897 and 896, do they realise that the next tens number will be 10 tens and so the new numbers will be 907 and 906?

Note

You could give extra practice at this by changing the parameters, for example between 600 and 700, and 700 and 800.

You could also make the link to fractions. The pupils should be introduced to tenths in the fractions requirements, so you could ask them to find the numbers between 80 and 90 using the three digits. Do they notice that, although the numbers have the same digits, they are 10 times smaller than the original numbers? If they do, they are showing a depth of mastery.

Number – Number and place value

Compare and order numbers

Challenge 5: Tom has been comparing different three-digit numbers. He wrote down his comparisons using the *is greater than*, *is less than* and *is equal to* symbols.

476 > 486   399 < 284   245 + 56 = 300   376 = 299 + 78

Do you agree with Tom? Explain your reasoning.

Challenge 6: Draw these three number lines on paper.

160_____250   175_____325   250_____434

Mark the number that can be found halfway along each of the number lines.

What numbers are they?

How do you know you are correct? Write an explanation. Prove it!

Identifying, representing and estimating numbers

Challenge 7: Fahmida represented 175 in different ways. She used coloured counters, money, her ruler, the bar model (to make a calculation about 175), and base 10 apparatus.

Her bar model looked like this:

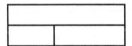

Can you show what each of her representations might have looked like?

Write an explanation for each representation.

Challenge 8: You need a container of counters – make sure there are a lot of them!

Estimate how many there are in the container. Write your estimate on paper.

Tip them onto the table and make another estimate. Write it down. Is it different from your original estimate?

Can you think of a good way to count them? Start counting!

When you are about halfway through counting, look at your estimate. If you want to change it, you can. When you have finished counting, compare the actual amount with your estimate. How close was it?

Write a sentence to explain your result. Are you good at estimating?

Challenge 5 Answer

All four of Tom's statements are incorrect.

Assessment

Ask the pupils to correct Tom's mistakes They should rewrite the statements.

For the first two, they should either change the symbol or swap the numbers, for example 476 < 486 or 486 > 476.

For the equivalence statements, ask them to provide two solutions: first, to write the *is greater than* or *is less than* symbol as appropriate (for example 245 + 56 > 300); and second to change a number in each statement to make the statements equal (for example 245 + 56 = 301 or 245 + 55 = 300).

Explanations should include definitions of the >, < and = symbols, for example, the *is equal to* symbol means that what is on one side of it must be equivalent in value to what is on the other. If any pupil thinks that the *is equal to* symbol means that a question is on one side and an answer is expected on the other, this misconception should be addressed – it simply means a balance; the two sides must have the same value.

Note

Ask pupils to make 476 > 486 and 399 < 284 equivalent in two different ways; for example 476 + 10 = 486 and 476 = 486 − 10. Do they notice that they need to add or subtract the same number to make the statements equal? If they can do this, they are showing a depth of mastery.

Challenge 6 Answer

160–––250: 205
175–––325: 250
250–––434: 342

Assessment

Assess the pupils' accuracy in drawing the number lines. Assess their fluency and reasoning skills according to the method they used to find the middle number.

The most efficient way would be to find the difference between the two given numbers, halve it and add it to the lesser number or subtract it from the greater number. Can they explain why this works? Or did they count on in equal steps from the lesser number and back in the same size steps from the greater number in order to get to the middle? This is an inefficient method which could lead to errors. If any pupils did this, it is an activity worth exploring with the whole class, beginning with numbers such as 140 and 220. Focus instead on finding the difference, halving and adding on to the lesser number.

Assess their explanation – is it clear? Encourage them to explain verbally to a partner. Can the partner understand the explanation and follow it to find their own middle number on a number line?

How did they prove they were correct? If they added half of the difference to the lesser number they could subtract it from the greater number and see if they get the same middle number. Or they could subtract the half from the middle number and see if they make the lesser number or add the half to the middle number to see if this makes the greater number. Proof is an important part of reasoning, and these skills need developing with all pupils.

You could ask them to find middle numbers between an odd number and an even number, such as 135 and 214. The difference will be odd, and so a number with half needs adding to the lesser number. For example, the difference between 135 and 214 is 79. Half of 79 is $39\frac{1}{2}$. So the middle number is $135 + 39\frac{1}{2} = 174\frac{1}{2}$. You could ask them to record the result in two ways; Year 3 pupils are introduced to tenths, so they could also record it as 174.5.

Challenge 7 Answer

If the pupils' explanations match their representations, then mark as correct. Look out for efficient representations.

Assessment

Have the pupils used three colours of counter? That is, one colour for the hundreds number, a second colour for the tens and a third for the ones. They should have 1 counter for the hundreds, 7 for the tens and 5 for the ones.

Do the pupils recognise that 175 could be represented as £1.75? Did they see that a £1 coin would represent the hundreds, seven 10p coins the tens, and five 1p coins the ones? Encourage them to look again and make the amount using the fewest coins: £1, 50p, 20p, 5p.

Do the pupils recognise that 175 could be represented as 17cm and 5mm? Ask them to draw a line of this length if they haven't already done so, and label it to assess their knowledge of centimetres and millimetres. Can they tell you that 17cm and 5mm is equivalent to 175mm?

When using the bar model, the longest bar should be 175, and then the two shorter bars any numbers that total 175. If any pupils have made one of the shorter bars 175, ask them to consider whether this is a good idea when the number they've been given is 175; they should be able to tell you that when adding the other value the minuend (a quantity or number from which another is to be subtracted) will be greater than 175. Ask the pupils to write the two commutative number statements that they can make, and the two inverse statements.

Assess how the pupils used the base 10 apparatus. Did they use the flat as 100, 7 tens sticks for 70, and 5 ones cubes for 5?

Note

The bar model is a key representation that should be embedded within the school. It is useful for problem solving as well as for making the generalisations involved in addition and subtraction. It would be worth using this model with the whole class.

Challenge 8 Answer

Dependent on the number of counters selected.

Assessment

Assess the pupils' ability to estimate. Does it appear to be sensible, and not a random guess? Are they willing to change their estimate when they have the counters on the table? It is often easier to make an estimate when items are spread out as opposed to being grouped together in a container.

Assess how the pupils approach the counting. Do they count one at a time or in twos or other groups? Once they have ten, do they keep them in a group and then count in, for example, twos to make another ten and set them aside? This would be an efficient way to count, as they could then count the tens and then count the extra ones.

Did they change their estimate about halfway through if they thought it was going to be too high or too low?

Can they assess if they are good at estimating?

Number – Number and place value

Reading and writing numbers up to 1000

Challenge 9: Match the numerals and the number words. There are some letters and some digits missing. You will need to work out what is missing first! Use the numbers in digits to help you.

a) _ _ _ hundred and _ _ e _ ty- _ _ _ r   **59_**

b) _ i _ e hundred and _ i _ ty- t _ _   **7_5**

c) _ _ _ _ _ hundred and _ _ _ ety- _ i _ e   **6_4**

d) _ _ _ hundred and _ _ g _ ty- _ _ _ _ _ _   **2_3**

e) _ i _ e hundred and _ i _ _ ty- _ _ e   **95_**

f) _ i _ _ _ hundred and _ i _ ty- _ i _ e   **_59**

Challenge 10: Tom had to write some numbers in words. He didn't do too well.

Can you show him how they are written correctly?

Can you also write how they look as numerals?

a) to hundred fivty sicks

b) ate hundred and atey and ate

c) for hundred twenty won

d) sicks hundred and thirty and for

e) seven hundred ninty and tree

Solving number problems and practical problems

Challenge 11: Is Fahmida correct? Explain your reasoning.

I can count back in steps of 4 from 224 and get to zero.

Challenge 12: Tom thinks that an odd number is an even number add one.

Is he correct? Prove it!

He also thinks that when you add two odd numbers the sum will be an even number.

Is he correct? Prove it!

Challenge 9 Answer

a)	six hundred and twenty-four	624
b)	nine hundred and fifty-two	952
c)	seven hundred and ninety-five	795
d)	two hundred and eighty-three	283
e)	five hundred and ninety-one	591
f)	eight hundred and fifty-nine	859

Assessment

Assess the pupils' ability to spell numbers in words accurately. Encourage them to learn how to spell any that they are not sure of. It might be a good idea to give these to them in spelling lists during English lessons.

Assess how the pupils work out the missing letters and digits in the numbers. Do they use their reasoning skills? For example, looking at the last item in the list, the only five-letter number with i as the second letter is eight, so that last number must be 859.

Can they make other deductions? For example, when looking at the third item with its five-letter hundreds number, only the words eight, seven or three could fit the space. Of the numerals given, 7 is the only possible one of these that appears in the hundreds position, so that word must be seven, and the number 795.

Ask the pupils to make up their own puzzles like this to give to their friends to solve.

Challenge 10 Answer

a)	two hundred and fifty-six	256
b)	eight hundred and eighty-eight	888
c)	four hundred and twenty-one	421
d)	six hundred and thirty-four	634
e)	seven hundred and ninety-three	793

Assessment

Assess the pupils' ability to spell numbers as words accurately. As mentioned in Challenge 9, encourage them to learn how to spell any that they are not sure of, and add these words to spelling lists in English.

Discuss how Tom had spelt the numbers. Establish that despite his ideas, most numbers are spelt as they sound. Discuss the way that he has used 'and'. Can any pupils tell you that 'and' is used to separate the hundred and tens numbers, and nowhere else?

Finally, assess how confident the pupils are at writing these numbers as numerals.

Challenge 11 Answer

Fahmida is correct. 224 is a multiple of 4 and therefore a count in fours to 224 will start at zero. Therefore counting back in fours will end at zero (if, as expected at this level, you are staying in positive numbers).

Assessment

Assess how the pupils find out if Fahmida is correct. There are several ways to do this. For example, they could have partitioned 224 into 200, 20 and 4; if they know that $5 \times 4 = 20$, they should know that $50 \times 4 = 200$.

Or they could have partitioned 224 into 200 and 24; if they know that $6 \times 4 = 24$, they can work out that $56 \times 4 = 224$.

Another way of finding out that 224 is a multiple of four would be to use the rule of divisibility for 4, which is that if the last two digits are a multiple of 4 then so is the whole number. In this number, 24 is a multiple of 4, so 224 must be as well.

Note

Exploring rules of divisibility is fun. You could do this with the whole class as part of a starter activity or for a whole lesson. It would be a way to rehearse multiplication facts for four. Write some three- and four-digit numbers on the board and ask the pupils to identify which are multiples of 4, for example, 730, 516, 408 and 3932. You could also explore the rules of divisibility for 3, 6 and 9.

Challenge 12 Answer

Tom is correct. An odd number is an even number add one. When you add two odd numbers the sum will be even.

Assessment

Assess the pupils as they carry out this task.

The first stage of proving this would be to take examples of odd numbers and break them down into an even number and one, for example, $7 = 6 + 1$, $19 = 18 + 1$.

They should work on a generalisation such as: if a number is n, to ensure it is even it would be $2n$, and to ensure it is an odd number it would be $2n + 1$; they may not express this in an algebraic format, but rather in their own words that convey the concept.

To prove that two odd numbers sum to an even number, they could start experimenting by adding pairs of odd numbers, for example $3 + 5 = 8$, $13 + 15 = 28$. They should then develop the generalisation that if an odd number is $2n + 1$ and another odd number is $2n + 1$, when they are added the result will always be $4n + 2$, proving that the result will always be an even number. Again, they will probably use their own words to express the concept.

Note

Making generalisations is a major part of reasoning and, as teachers, we should always look out for opportunities for pupils to develop this skill.

Number – Addition and subtraction

Adding and subtracting mentally

Challenge 1: Fahmida has added these numbers using different mental calculation strategies.

a) 234 + 16 = 230 + 20 = 250

b) 365 + 19 = 365 + 20 − 1 = 384

c) 444 + 21 = 444 + 20 + 1 = 465

d) 345 + 18 = 350 + 13 = 363

e) 150 + 151 = 150 × 2 + 1 = 301

What mental calculation strategies has she used? Explain your reasoning in writing.

Challenge 2: Tom worked out the answers to some calculations. He made some mistakes.
Can you find them? Explain what he could have done wrong.

a) 456 + 30 = 756

b) 614 + 7 = 611

c) 789 + 20 = 7109

d) 555 − 10 = 455

e) 150 − 9 = 159

Adding

Challenge 3:

I can use the column method to answer 256 + 240. That is the only way I know.

There are other methods that Tom can use.

How many can you think of? Try to think of two other ways.

Write explanations of what you could do.

Challenge 4: Solve these:

a)
```
    2   4   □
+   3   □   6
─────────────
    6   3   1
```

b)
```
    5   □   4
+   □   7   6
─────────────
    9   4   0
```

c)
```
    7   □   3
+   □   5   9
─────────────
    9   3   □
```

d)
```
    6   □   7
+   2   7   □
─────────────
□   0   9
```

e)
```
    4   5   7
+   □   □ □
─────────────
    7   8   6
```

f)
```
    3   □   6
+   2   6   □
─────────────
□   5   3
```

Explain how you managed to find the missing digits. Now you know all the numbers, find the answers using a different method.

National Curriculum objective, Year 3, Addition and subtraction

- **add and subtract numbers mentally, including:**
  - *a three-digit number and ones*
  - *a three-digit number and tens*
  - *a three-digit number and hundreds*

Challenge 1 Answer

Accept answers that fit with what Fahmida has done.

a) $234 + 16 = 230 + 20 = 250$: using number bonds to 10

b) $365 + 19 = 365 + 20 - 1 = 384$: rounding and adjusting

c) $444 + 21 = 444 + 20 + 1 = 465$: sequencing

d) $345 + 18 = 350 + 13 = 363$: bridging 10

e) $150 + 151 = 150 \times 2 + 1 = 301$: near doubles

Assessment

Assess the explanations that the pupils have written. Do they match the ways Fahmida has broken down her calculations? These are well-known mental calculation strategies that the pupils need to be taught.

Note

In the National Curriculum, pupils are required to perform the four operations mentally, but there is no guidance on how to do this. This activity seeks to remedy that lack; the mental calculation strategies shown above are useful ones. It is important to teach these so that the pupils can decide on efficient methods to use when adding and subtracting. For every calculation, they need to think: 'Can I do this in my head, or would using jottings or a written method be more efficient?'

Once written methods are taught, many pupils rely on using these even when they are not necessary. So we need to help pupils to think flexibly. It might be a good idea to spend a week working on mental calculation strategies before teaching written methods.

Challenge 2 Answer

All Tom's answers were incorrect.

a) $456 + 30 = 756$: he added 300 instead of 30. If he'd added 30 he'd have got the correct answer, 486.

b) $614 + 7 = 611$: he added 7 to 4 to give 11, but he didn't exchange the 10 ones for a ten. If he'd done that he'd have got the correct answer, 621.

c) $789 + 20 = 7109$: he added 20 to 80 to make 100 – but he didn't exchange the 10 tens for 100 and add that to the 700. If he'd done that he'd have got the correct answer, 809.

d) $555 - 10 = 455$: he took away 100 instead of 10. If he'd taken 10 away, he'd have got the correct answer, 545.

e) $150 - 9 = 159$: he added instead of subtracting. If he'd subtracted the 9, he'd have got the correct answer, 141.

Assessment

Assess whether the pupils can identify each error and if their explanations clearly show what he has done wrong. Ask the pupils to show what the answers should have been.

- *add and subtract numbers with up to three digits, using formal written methods of columnar addition and subtraction*

Challenge 3 Answer

Tom could have used, for example, sequencing or doubling as alternative methods. Some further methods are listed in the answer to Challenge 1. Any method for a mental calculation strategy that has been explained and gives the correct answer is acceptable.

Assessment

Assess whether the pupils can use a variety of mental calculation strategies to answer this.

Discuss with them whether they think the written column method is efficient. If they think it is, a focus on mental calculation is probably necessary in your whole-class teaching. Did any pupils think of sequencing (256 + 200 + 40 = 496)? What about doubling (240 + 240 + 16 = 496)?

Challenge 4 Answer

a)	b)	c)	d)	e)	f)
24**5**	564	773	637	457	386
+ 38**6**	+ **3**76	+ **1**59	+ 272	+ **3**29	+ 267
631	940	93**2**	**9**09	786	**6**53

Assessment

Assess whether the pupils can identify the missing digits. Discuss with them how they would go about doing this. Expect them to take each column in turn, beginning with the ones. They should be able to work out the missing ones digit quite easily.

Most of the calculations involve at least one exchange. Do they remember to adjust the missing digits in the tens and hundreds positions correctly?

What other methods do they use to calculate the additions? Look out for mental calculation strategies such as sequencing or bridging 10. If any pupils have simply used commutativity, ask them to find another way as well. If they have subtracted (used inversion) remind them that this could be used as a check but they still need to add the original augend (the number to which another is needed) and addend (a number which is added to another).

Note

Bridging 10 is a great mental calculation strategy which should be taught to the whole class, with simpler numbers initially. For example, adding 19 and 16. To round the 19 up to 20 needs 1, so take 1 from the 16 and add it to the 19. This makes the calculation 20 + 15 = 35.

Then try with more complex numbers, such as 245 + 386. To round the 386 up to the nearest 10 needs 4, so take 4 from the 245 and add it to the 386. This makes the calculation 241 + 390. Then to round the 390 up to 400 needs 10, so take 10 from the 241 and add it to the 390. This makes the calculation 231 + 400. This is now very simple to add.

Number — Addition and subtraction

Subtracting

Challenge 5:

I can use the column method to answer 548 – 299. That is the only way I know.

There are other methods that Tom can use.

How many can you think of? Try to think of two other ways.

Write explanations of what you could do.

Challenge 6: Solve these:

a)
```
    4  5  6
 –  2  3  □
 ─────────
    □  1  9
```

b)
```
    □  7  3
 –  4  □  1
 ─────────
    1  9  □
```

c)
```
    5  □  2
 –  □  6  4
 ─────────
    2  6  □
```

d)
```
    8  3  5
 –  4  □  □
 ─────────
    □  6  1
```

e)
```
    6  4  □
 –  2  □  9
 ─────────
    □  5  2
```

Explain how you managed to find the missing digits.

Now you know all the numbers, find the answers to these subtraction calculations using a different method.

Estimating

Challenge 7:

486 + 398

I think the answer to this calculation is about 700. That's my estimate!

Explain how Fahmida has made her estimate.

Do you agree with her? If not, what would your estimate be?

Write an explanation of your thinking.

Challenge 8: Estimate the answers to these calculations.

a) 215 + 398   b) 399 – 275   c) 675 + 289   d) 602 – 278

Now find the actual answers.

How close were your estimates?

National Curriculum objective, Year 3, Addition and subtraction

- add and subtract numbers mentally, including:
  - a three-digit number and ones
  - a three-digit number and tens
  - a three-digit number and hundreds
- add and subtract numbers with up to three digits, using formal written methods of columnar addition and subtraction

Challenge 5 Answer

Tom could have used, for example, rounding and adjusting or counting on. He could also have made the calculation simpler. Any method that has been explained by the pupils and gives the correct answer is acceptable.

Assessment

Discuss with pupils whether they think the column written method is efficient for these particular numbers. If they think it is, a focus on mental calculation is probably necessary in your whole-class teaching.

Assess the calculation strategies that the pupils used. Were these carried out efficiently, fluently and accurately?

Did any pupils think of rounding and adjusting (548 – 300 + 1 = 249)? What about counting on (299 + 1 + 248)? Did any make the calculation simpler by adding 1 to each number to make 549 – 300? It might be worth working on this strategy with your class. If adding or subtracting the same number to the minuend (a quantity or number from which another is to be subtracted) and subtrahend (a quantity or number to be subtracted from another), the difference will always be the same.

Challenge 6 Answer

a)		b)		c)		d)		e)	
	456		673		532		835		641
	− 237		− 481		− 264		− 474		− 289
	219		192		268		361		352

Assessment

Assess whether the pupils can identify the missing digits. Discuss with them how they would go about doing this. Expect them to take each column in turn, beginning with the ones. They should be able to work out the missing ones digit quite easily.

All of the calculations involve at least one exchange. Did they remember to adjust the missing digits in the tens and hundreds positions correctly to allow for the exchanges?

Encourage pupils to check their results using the inverse operation or a mental calculation strategy. Look out for mental calculation strategies, such as sequencing or counting on. Did any pupils make the calculation simpler, for example adding 19 to 673 and 481 to make the calculation 692 – 500?

Discuss with them how efficient these strategies are for subtraction calculations like these. They might be for some, but for others it might be more efficient to use the written method.

Note

Making a subtraction simpler by adding or subtracting the same number to or from both the minuend and the subtrahend is a great strategy. We are finding the difference between the two, so if we add or subtract the same number to both we are changing the *values* but not the *difference*. For example, 532 – 264 = 268; if we add 36 to both numbers we make the simpler calculation 568 – 300, and the difference is still 268. Of course, this relies on pupils being fluent with number bonds to 10, 20 and 100; if they are not, this might be an area that needs to be focused on.

National Curriculum objective, Year 3, Addition and subtraction

- *estimate the answer to a calculation*

Challenge 7 Answer

Fahmida's estimate is a little low. She has added the hundreds digits together for her estimate. A closer estimate would be given if the numbers are rounded to the nearest 100 (500 and 400) to give an estimate of 900.

Assessment

Assess the pupils' ability to round numbers to the nearest 100 to give an estimate of 900. If they cannot round, or do so without confidence, you may need to work on this during whole-class mathematics lessons.

Did any pupils make a closer estimate by rounding to the nearest 10? 486 + 398 could be rounded to 490 and 400 to give an estimate of 890. Pupils giving this estimate would be showing a deeper level of mastery.

Note

Rounding is an important skill. It is useful for finding approximate totals or differences which we often do in real life with money and also for the mental calculation strategy of rounding and adjusting.

Challenge 8 Answer

To make their estimates, the pupils should have rounded to the nearest 100 or 10.

a) 215 + 398: round to 200 + 400 = 600, or 220 + 400 = 620

Actual answer: 613

b) 399 − 275: round to 400 − 300 = 100, or 400 − 280 = 120

Actual answer: 124

c) 675 + 289: round to 700 + 300 = 1000, or 680 + 290 = 970

Actual answer: 964

d) 602 − 278: round to 600 − 300 = 300, or 600 − 280 = 320

Actual answer: 324

Assessment

Assess whether the pupils can estimate by rounding to the nearest 10; this shows a deeper understanding than rounding to 100. If they have simply rounded to 100, ask them if they can make a more accurate estimate.

Assess how the pupils found the actual answers. Did they think carefully about whether they could use a mental calculation strategy, or whether it would be more efficient to use a written method? For example, 399 − 275 could be answered by sequencing: 399 − 200 − 70 − 5. A written method is not as efficient.

Note

Ensure that you give pupils opportunities to rehearse and use mental calculation strategies, because these are very important.

Written methods are not always the most efficient. You might need to consider the calculations that you give to pupils to answer, and allow them to decide which methods are most appropriate.

Number – Addition and subtraction

Inverse operations

Challenge 9:

I've used the bar model to show the relationship between addition and subtraction.

300	125
175	

Is Fahmida correct? Explain your reasoning.

Draw your own bar model for this set of numbers: 165, 384 and 219.

Now write the two commutative statements and the two inverse statements.

Make up some more bar models and statements of your own.

Challenge 10: Explain in writing what Tom means.

Make up some examples to prove your explanation.

I can check the answer to a subtraction by using the inverse operation.

Solving problems

Challenge 11: Solve these missing number calculations.

a) ☐ + 254 = 487   b) 267 + ☐ = 584

c) ☐ − 267 = 154   d) 354 − ☐ = 213

Explain how you knew what to do.

Draw each calculation using a bar model. How does this help?

Make up some missing number statements like these for a friend to solve.

Challenge 12: Draw a bar model to show this problem.

When you have worked out the answer, write the two addition and the two subtraction facts.

I had 245 marbles and gave 167 to my friend. Can you work out how many marbles I had left?

What if Tom gave 98 marbles to his friend? What if he gave 139 to his friend?

Make up some other amounts that he could have given to his friend, and find out how many he had left.

Challenge 9 Answer

Fahmida is incorrect; her bar model should have looked like this:

175	125
300	

The pupils' bar model should be:

219	165
384	

The commutative and inverse statements are:

219 + 165 = 384

165 + 219 = 384

384 – 165 = 219

384 – 219 = 165

The long bar can be at the top or the bottom in all cases.

Assessment

Assess to see if the pupils can identify what Fahmida has done wrong.

Can they identify that 300 is the largest number and so must go into the longest bar? Do they understand the part / part whole element of the bar model, and realise that it doesn't matter which way round the bars are drawn?

Can the pupils use the bar model to show the relationship between addition and subtraction?

Do they understand commutativity and inverse? If not, this is something that you will need to work on with the whole class.

Note

The bar model is an effective tool to help pupils solve problems. It shows the underlying structure of the problem, and makes knowns and unknowns obvious. It isn't a calculating tool; pupils still need to do the arithmetic. If you haven't already done so, make sure that the use of bar models is embedded into your teaching.

Challenge 10 Answer

Tom is correct; one way to check the answer to a subtraction is to use the inverse operation of addition. Expect pupils to explain that subtraction is the inverse operation to addition, so Tom could have checked a solution by adding the difference to the subtrahend (a quantity or number to be subtracted from another) to make the minuend (a quantity or number from which another is to be subtracted).

Assessment

Assess the clarity of pupils' explanations. Encourage them to read their explanation to a friend. Can their friend understand the explanation?

Assess their examples and encourage them to write the associated two addition and two subtraction statements. Do they use a bar model?

Note

It would be a good idea to practise these ideas using measures such as money or length, so that pupils understand that the process is the same no matter what type of numbers are used.

- *solve problems, including missing number problems, using number facts, place value, and more complex addition and subtraction*

Challenge 11 Answer

a) **233** + 254 = 487

b) 267 + **317** = 584

c) **421** − 267 = 154

d) 354 − **141** = 213

The bar models for these calculations would look like this:

233	254
487	

267	317
584	

421	
267	154

354	
141	213

The long bar can be at the top or the bottom in all cases.

Assessment

Assess how pupils found the missing numbers. Did they use a mental calculation strategy if appropriate, for example sequencing or counting on? Did they use written methods appropriately?

Assess the pupils' ability to clearly explain their reasoning about how to use a bar model.

Note

You may need to give pupils regular opportunities to answer missing-number questions like these.

Challenge 12 Answer

245 − 167 = 78
245 − 78 = 167
167 + 78 = 245
78 + 167 = 245

If Tom gave 98 marbles to his friend he would have 147 left.

If he gave 139 marbles to his friend he would have 106 left.

Assessment

Assess the pupils' use of the bar model to help them understand what the problem is asking them to do. If they do not do this automatically, spend some time teaching the class this model.

Do they notice what is similar and what is different about the later problems? (The problem is the same, and the minuend is the same – it is the subtrahend, and therefore the result, that is different each time.)

Note

Variation is an important part of practice. We can give pupils cognitive overload by asking them to practise word problems that are completely different from one another, with totally different numbers to manipulate. Variation is about keeping most things the same and changing just one aspect. If you don't already embed variation into your teaching practice, aim to do so.

Number – Multiplication and division

Multiplication and division facts

Challenge 1:

> I know that 7 multiplied by 8 equals 56. Because I know that, I know loads more facts!

Do you agree with Tom? Explain your reasoning on paper.

Give examples of what else Tom could know.

Challenge 2:

> Multiplication is commutative, and division is the inverse of multiplication.

What does Fahmida mean by 'commutative' and 'inverse'?

Write a definition for each word, with some examples.

Using multiplication facts

Challenge 3:

> I know my multiplication facts up to 12 × 4. I therefore know my multiplication facts up to 12 × 8.

Why does knowing facts up to 12 × 4 help Fahmida to know her facts up to 12 × 8?

Explain your reasoning in writing. Write all the facts to 12 × 4 and 12 × 8 to show the patterns.

Challenge 4: You need 24 counters. Make as many different arrays as you can. Draw them.

Write the two multiplication and two division statements for each array.

Explain to a friend what you have done. Convince them that you have found them all.

National Curriculum objective, Year 3, Multiplication and division

- *recall and use multiplication and division facts for the 3, 4 and 8 multiplication tables*

Challenge 1 Answer

Yes, Tom is correct; he can make up many facts from 7 × 8 = 56. For example, 7 × 80 = 560, 70 × 80 = 5600, 35 × 80 = 2800, 35 × 40 = 1400, 35 × 20 = 700.

Assessment

How many facts do the pupils make up? Expect them to produce at least 15 new facts. Assess how they made them. Encourage them to multiply and divide by 10, and to double and halve. Assess their fluency. Can they make new facts quickly, using what they already know?

Note

Using what we already know is an effective mental calculation strategy, and one that needs embedding with all pupils. You could do activities such as this one during lesson starters or warm-ups, or whenever you have a few spare minutes during the day.

Challenge 2 Answer

'Commutative' means that it doesn't matter which way round you multiply numbers together; for example 12 × 8 = 96 and 8 × 12 = 96. Whichever way round you put the numbers you're multiplying, the answer will always be the same. 'Inverse' here means that division is the reverse of multiplication; for example, 96 ÷ 8 = 12, 96 ÷ 12 = 8.

Assessment

Assess the pupils' clarity when they are explaining commutativity and inverse. Ensure that they give two or three suitable examples.

Note

The relationship between multiplication and division is very important, as is commutativity. Arrays are perfect models for seeing how the two operations fit together, for example:

This array clearly shows that:

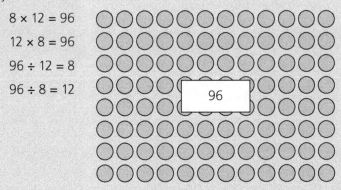

8 × 12 = 96
12 × 8 = 96
96 ÷ 12 = 8
96 ÷ 8 = 12

96

Challenge 3 Answer

Multiplication facts for 8 are double those for 4. So if Fahmida knows the facts up to 12 × 4, she can double each answer to find facts up to 12 × 8.

Assessment

Do the pupils make the link between multiplying by 4 and multiplying by 8? Assess how fluent they are with their multiplication facts up to 12 × 4. If they are not fluent, ensure you give them opportunities to practise instant recall of these facts.

Observe the pupils to see if they can make all the facts to 12 × 8 by doubling. Assess how fluent the pupils are with their multiplication facts up to 12 × 8. If they are not fluent, instant recall of these will need practising.

Note

Knowing multiplication facts is important. They are useful when solving problems involving multiplication and division and also when working with fractions. Practise whichever facts the pupils need to work on regularly, and make them a focus for multiplication and division. For example, if the pupils are learning the facts for 8, multiply and divide all numbers by 8 so that they are immersed in facts for 8 and stand a good chance of remembering them.

Challenge 4 Answer

Arrays should show 1 × 24, 2 × 12, 3 × 8 and 4 × 6.

Some pupils might also show 24 × 1, 12 × 2, 8 × 3, 6 × 4, but these are not necessary because their written statements should include the commutative facts:

1 × 24 = 24, 24 × 1 = 24, 24 ÷ 1 = 24, 24 ÷ 24 = 1

2 × 12 = 24, 12 × 2 = 24, 24 ÷ 2 = 12, 24 ÷ 12 = 2

3 × 8 = 24, 8 × 3 = 24, 24 ÷ 3 = 8, 24 ÷ 8 = 3

4 × 6 = 24, 6 × 4 = 24, 24 ÷ 4 = 6, 24 ÷ 6 = 4

Assessment

Assess the pupils as they make their arrays. Do they show an understanding of commutativity by telling you that they could simply turn each of their four arrays around to show the commutative facts?

Do they understand that division is the inverse of multiplication? Can they see from their array that, for example, you can take four groups of 6 away from 24, and also six groups of 4?

Note

Commutativity and inverse are generalisations that all pupils need to understand. It is worth spending time looking at these for all four operations.

Number – Multiplication and division

Mental calculation strategies

Challenge 5:

I can multiply two-digit numbers by 5 by multiplying them by 10 and halving the answer.

Is Fahmida correct? Explain your reasoning with examples.

Challenge 6:

I can multiply two-digit numbers by 8 by doubling, doubling and doubling again.

Is Tom correct? Explain your reasoning with examples.

Solving problems with multiplication and division

Challenge 7: Fahmida has some books. Tom has four times as many.

The difference between the number of books they have is 72.

What is the sum of their books?

Fahmida's books

Here is a model of the problem: Tom's books

Explain to a friend how you worked this out. Now write an explanation.

Make up similar problems. Keep the problem the same, but vary the differences in the number of books. What do you notice about the difference each time?

Challenge 8: Tom has 8 bags with 24 marbles in each bag.

Fahmida has 4 bags with 36 marbles in each bag.

How many marbles do they have altogether?

Explain your reasoning.

Make up similar problems. Keep the problem the same, but vary the number of Tom's marbles.

National Curriculum objective, Year 3, Multiplication and division

- *write and calculate mathematical statements for multiplication and division using the multiplication tables that they know, including for two-digit numbers times one-digit numbers, using mental and progressing to formal written methods*

Challenge 5 Answer

Fahmida is correct; 5 is half of 10, so multiplying by 10 and then halving is a good strategy for multiplying by 5. Ensure the pupils show examples, such as 28 × 5: 28 × 10 = 280, half 280 = 140, so 28 × 5 = 140.

Assessment

Do pupils really understand what happens to a number when it is multiplied by 10? It is important that they never refer to adding a zero. They need to use their knowledge of the base 10 aspect of place value. This is that our number system increases and decreases in powers of 10. When a number, for example 28, is multiplied by 10, each digit becomes 10 times greater. So the 8 becomes 80, and the 20 becomes 200, and a 0 is positioned in the ones place (or column) as a place-holder. Can pupils use this strategy successfully?

Note

This way of multiplying a number by 5 is a good mental calculation strategy to teach. It might be worth teaching it to the whole class. But while we're encouraging our pupils to use this mental calculation strategy, it also means that when we're focusing on the written method we need to avoid selecting 5 as a multiplier.

Challenge 6 Answer

Tom is correct. Doubling is the same as multiplying by 2, doubling twice is the same as multiplying by 4, and doubling three times is the same as multiplying by 8. Pupils should give their own examples of multiplying by 8 in this way, for example, 36 × 8: 36, 72, 144, 288. So 36 × 8 = 288.

Assessment

Do pupils understand that they can multiply by 8 using this strategy, and why? Expect them to be able to tell you that double 1 is 2, double 2 is 4, and double 4 is 8, so doubling three times is the same as multiplying by 8.

Assess their doubling skills. Can they do this completely mentally, or do they make jottings? Making jottings is fine; we don't always need to expect pupils to hold all information in their heads.

Note

Multiplying small numbers by 8 in this way is a good mental calculation strategy to teach. It might be worth teaching it to the whole class.

National Curriculum objective, Year 3, Multiplication and division

- *write and calculate mathematical statements for multiplication and division using the multiplication tables that they know, including for two-digit numbers times one-digit numbers, using mental and progressing to formal written methods*

Challenge 7 Answer

Using the drawing in the question, we can see that the difference of 72 is represented by three circles. So we divide 72 by 3 to give the value of each circle, which is 24.

The sum of the circles is 5, so we multiply 24 by 5 (which we can do by multiplying by 10 and then halving) to give 120. So the sum of their books is 120.

Assessment

Assess the clarity of the pupils' explanation as to why they have a sum of 120. Do they know what is meant by 'sum'? Many people use this word informally to mean 'calculation', but its more precise meaning is 'the answer to an addition calculation'. It is important that the pupils understand this specific meaning, and use it in arithmetic.

How do the pupils divide 72 by 3? Do they partition 72 into 60 and 12 and use their multiplication facts, for example $2 \times 3 = 6$, so $20 \times 3 = 60$?

Assess the problems that they made up. Did they notice the fact that the difference must be a multiple of 3?

Challenge 8 Answer

Tom has 192 marbles. Fahmida has 144 marbles. Altogether they have 336.

Assessment

Assess the clarity of the explanation as to why they have 336 marbles altogether.

How did they multiply by 4 and 8? Did they use the doubling strategy? Can they explain it to you?

What other strategies did they use? Discuss other possibilities, for example partitioning and multiplying each part by 4 and 8, and then recombining. If using this strategy, 24 would be partitioned into 20 and 4. Then 20 would be multiplied by 8, by using what we already know ($2 \times 8 = 16$, so $20 \times 8 = 160$), and 4 would be multiplied by 8, using multiplication facts, to make 32; adding the two products, 160 and 32, gives 192.

Could they make up and solve their own problems by simply changing the number of marbles in each of Tom's bags?

Note

Variation is an important aspect of mastery. Variation is a small step change so that the pupils don't have cognitive overload by having too much that is different, for example a different problem and different numbers to manipulate. It would be a good idea to plan variation into teaching sequences so that, for example, the problem is the same and one of the numbers varies, or the numbers stay the same and the context of the problem varies.

Number – Multiplication and division

Missing number problems

Challenge 9: Fahmida was having trouble solving some missing number problems.

Can you help her out?

m stands for the missing number.

a) $m \times 8 = 240$ **b)** $32 \times m = 160$ **c)** $m \div 4 = 25$

d) $96 \div m = 16$ **e)** $90 \div m = 6 \times 3$ **f)** $m \times 4 = 10 \times 8$

Explain to a friend how you worked these out. Now write an explanation.

Make up some more missing number problems for your friend to answer. You need to answer them first to make sure that they are correct!

Challenge 10: Find the missing multipliers in these calculations.

The missing numbers are shown by the letter *m*.

a) $24 \times m = 72$ **b)** $53 \times m = 159$ **c)** $39 \times m = 234$

d) $57 \times m = 342$ **e)** $28 \times m = 224$ **f)** $48 \times m = 384$

Show what these would look like using manipulatives. Translate that to the grid method.

What is the same about all the representations? What is different?

Scaling

Challenge 11: Tom had a piece of rope. It was 75cm in length.

Fahmida also had a piece of rope. Her piece was five times longer than Tom's.

How many centimetres longer was Fahmida's piece of rope than Tom's?

Draw a model to show this problem.

Now write an explanation of what you did to solve it. What if Tom's piece of rope is 110cm in length? What if it is 124cm in length?

Challenge 12: Fahmida had a collection of stamps. Her collection was a quarter the size of Tom's.

If Tom had 96 stamps, how many did they have altogether?

Draw a model to show this problem. Now write an explanation of what you did to solve it. What if Tom had 132 stamps? What if he had 172 stamps?

National Curriculum objective, Year 3, Multiplication and division

- *solve problems, including missing number problems, involving multiplication and division*

Challenge 9 Answer

a) $30 \times 8 = 240$

b) $32 \times 5 = 160$

c) $100 \div 4 = 25$

d) $96 \div 6 = 16$

e) $90 \div 5 = 6 \times 3$

f) $20 \times 4 = 10 \times 8$

Assessment

Assess the clarity of the explanation as to what the missing numbers are. How did the pupils work these out? Can you tell from their explanations? Discuss their methods with them to see if they have used what they already know; for example, there are 3 groups of 8 in 24 so there must be 30 groups of 8 in 240.

Were they able to make up and solve their own missing number problems? Was their friend able to solve them too?

Note

Focus on using what you already know as a mental calculation strategy. It will help the pupils becomes flexible thinkers.

Make links to measures. You could ask the pupils to work on the problems again, with the numbers as money. They could, for example, collect 30p using the fewest coins, eight times – and then work out the total to see if it is £2.40.

Challenge 10 Answer

a) $24 \times 3 = 72$

b) $53 \times 3 = 159$

c) $39 \times 6 = 234$

d) $57 \times 6 = 342$

e) $28 \times 8 = 224$

f) $48 \times 8 = 384$

Assessment

Assess how the pupils found the multipliers. Did they make sensible estimates of what they could have been and worked from their estimates? Pupils are often reluctant to estimate. The skill would be really helpful in missing-number questions. Did they partition the numbers to see if that would help? For example, 53 can be partitioned into 50 and 3.

What would the multiplier be to give 150 and 9? They should be able to see clearly that it must be 3. Can they partition numbers in different ways that would be helpful? For example, partitioning 72 into different numbers of tens (70 and 2, 60 and 12, 50 and 22, 40 and 32, etc.) would help them deduce that with 60 and 12 the multiplier must be 3. They could find out roughly how many of the minuends (a quantity or number from which another is to be subtracted) will fit into the product using estimates; for example, there are 6 groups of 40 in 240, so it makes sense that 39 would be multiplied by 6 to give 234.

Assess the pupils' confidence at setting each calculation out using manipulatives such as base 10 or place-value counters. Can they set these out as arrays and then draw the grid method from their model?

Assess their confidence in talking about the similarities and differences about the three models, for example, same calculation, different appearance.

Note

You could make links to measures. Ask the pupils to show the completed calculations using money. They could write down what coins they would collect to make, for example, three lots of 24p, and then work out the total to see if it is 72p.

Challenge 11 Answer

Fahmida's rope was 300cm or 3m longer than Tom's.

If Tom's rope is 110cm, Fahmida's is 440cm or 4m 40cm longer. If Tom's is 124cm, Fahmida's is 496cm or 4m 96cm longer.

Assessment

Assess how the pupils have drawn the model for this problem. Have they drawn a bar model? For example:

Tom's rope	75cm				
Fahmida's rope	75cm	75cm	75cm	75cm	75cm

Can they use their model to identify the 4 parts of Fahmida's rope that are more than Tom's? Assess the strategy they used to find four lots of 75cm. Ideally they would have used doubling. They could have partitioned the number into 70cm and 5cm, doubled them both twice (once for 2 and a second time for 4) and then recombined.

Were they able to replicate this for the other two questions, which were a variation? The only change was the length of Tom's rope. What do they notice about the examples? Essentially the problems are asking the same thing, so the mathematics is the same. The numbers are different. Did any of them find an alternative way to find the second pair of answers? For example, when Tom's rope was 110cm – that is, 35cm longer than 75cm – the pupils could have found four lots of 35cm (140cm) and added it to the four original lots of 75cm (300cm), to total 440.

Ask pupils to make up their own problems using variation of the first problem.

Challenge 12 Answer

Fahmida had 24 stamps, so they had 120 altogether.
If Tom had 132 stamps, Fahmida would have 33, so they would have 165 altogether.
If he had 172 stamps, Fahmida would have 43, so they would have 215 altogether.

Assessment

Assess how the pupils have drawn the model for this problem. Have they drawn a bar model? For example:

96 stamps

Can they use their model to identify that Fahmida has a quarter of the amount that Tom has? So Fahmida has one part for Tom's four. Did they realise that they needed to divide the whole of Tom's number of stamps by 4 to find one part, or one quarter, which is equivalent to the number of stamps that Fahmida has? Assess the strategy they used to find one quarter. Ideally, they would have halved and halved again, or used their knowledge of multiplication facts. They could have partitioned 96 into two numbers that can be halved easily, for example 80 and 16, then halved them both twice (once for dividing by 2 and a second time for dividing by 4) and then recombined.

How did they find out how many altogether? There are five parts in total, so they could have multiplied by 10 and halved. Were they able to replicate this for the other two questions, which were a variation on the first problem? What do they notice about the examples? Essentially the problems are asking the same thing, so the mathematics is the same. The numbers are different. Ask pupils to make up their own problems using variation.

Note

It is important that pupils understand that numbers can be partitioned in different ways, not simply the usual tens and ones. Doing this will help the pupils see how to make numbers easier to manipulate.

Correspondence problems

Challenge 13: Fahmida has four T-shirts and three pairs of shorts that she likes to wear in the summer.

Is Fahmida correct? Explain your reasoning.

Think of a way that you can clearly record the number of different outfits Fahmida can wear.

Challenge 14: Tom knows that multiplication is commutative, but he thinks that division is, too.

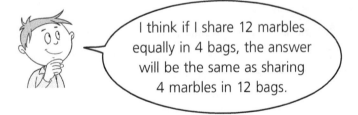

Do you agree with Tom?

Explain your reasoning. Draw diagrams to help explain this clearly.

Challenge 13 Answer

Fahmida is not exactly correct. She can make as many as 12 different outfits.

Assessment

Assess how the pupils have recorded how to find the different outfits. For example:

	T-shirt 1	T-shirt 2	T-shirt 3	T-shirt 4
Shorts 1	x	x	x	x
Shorts 2	x	x	x	x
Shorts 3	x	x	x	x

T-shirt 1 × 3 shorts = 3 outfits

T-shirt 2 × 3 shorts = 3 outfits

T-shirt 3 × 3 shorts = 3 outfits

T-shirt 4 × 3 shorts = 3 outfits

Total   = 12 outfits

Does pupils' reasoning agree with their recording? Assess their understanding of how problems like these are multiplication problems. Can they tell you that there are 4 T-shirts that can go with each of 3 pairs of shorts?

Note

These ideas are in 'Notes and guidance', under the National Curriculum requirements, and could easily be missed. We need to make sure we give pupils the opportunity to solve them. They lead well into future algebra.

Challenge 14 Answer

Tom is not correct; division is *not* commutative.

Assessment

Assess the pupils' understanding of multiplication and division and the relationship between them.

Can they explain what 'commutative' means, and do they understand that knowing this helps in learning multiplication facts? If they know one multiplication fact, then they need to realise that they know a second; for example, if they know 7 × 8 = 56 then they automatically know that 8 × 7 = 56.

Can they tell you that, even though division is the inverse of multiplication, it is *not* commutative? That is, does their reasoning explanation highlight that, while sharing 12 marbles in 4 bags gives 3 marbles in each bag, it is not possible to share 4 marbles in 12 bags? There are not enough marbles.

Look out for pupils who draw repeated addition bars to show that there will be 3 marbles in each bag or who divide their bar into 4 equal parts. For example:

12			
3	3	3	3

Look out for explanations and diagrams that show 4 wholes shared into 12 parts altogether would give thirds. This shows mastery with greater depth.

1			2			3			4		
$\frac{1}{3}$	$\frac{1}{3}$	$\frac{1}{3}$	$\frac{1}{3}$	$\frac{1}{3}$	$\frac{1}{3}$	$\frac{1}{3}$	$\frac{1}{3}$	$\frac{1}{3}$	$\frac{1}{3}$	$\frac{1}{3}$	$\frac{1}{3}$

Note

These ideas are in 'Notes and guidance', under the National Curriculum requirements, and could easily be missed. We need to make sure we give pupils the opportunity to solve them. They link well to fractions.

Number – Fractions

Tenths

Challenge 1:

I can count in tenths. When I have counted 100 tenths I will have counted 10 wholes.

Prove that Tom is correct.

Explain your reasoning on paper.

Challenge 2:

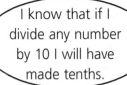

I know that if I divide any number by 10 I will have made tenths.

Is Fahmida always, sometimes or never correct?

Explain your reasoning on paper. Give examples to show what you mean.

Finding fractions

Challenge 3:

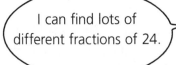

I can find lots of different fractions of 24.

How many fractions of 24 can you make?

Use counters. Make your fractions, draw what you have done, and write some sentences to show what you have drawn.

Challenge 4: You will need four strips of paper. Keep one whole. Fold one in half. Fold another in half twice. Fold the last one in half three times.

Write the fractions you have made inside each part.

Draw what you have made.

If the whole is one hour, what are all the parts?

If the whole is one kilogram, what are all the parts?

National Curriculum objective, Year 3, Fractions

- *count up and down in tenths; recognise that tenths arise from dividing an object into 10 equal parts and in dividing one-digit numbers or quantities by 10*

Challenge 1 Answer

Tom is correct: 10 tenths is equivalent to one whole, 20 tenths to two wholes up to 100 tenths, which make 10 wholes.

Assessment

During the task, assess whether the pupils understand tenths – that one-tenth arises when 1 is divided by 10.

Assess whether they can tell you that 10 tenths make one whole. Can they use this knowledge to explain that 20 tenths would be equivalent to two wholes, 30 would be three and so on, until they reach 100 tenths being equivalent to 10 wholes?

Assess to see if they have made this clear in their explanations. Have they given examples such as $\frac{10}{10} = 1$, $\frac{20}{10} = 2$, $\frac{30}{10} = 3$, $\frac{40}{10} = 4$, $\frac{50}{10} = 5$ and so on? What patterns can they see? Can they predict what 120 tenths would be? Ask them to tell you that 15 tenths would be equivalent to $1\frac{5}{10}$ or $1\frac{1}{2}$. Can they see the equivalence between $\frac{5}{10}$ and $\frac{1}{2}$?

Can they tell you the generalisation for equivalent fractions? Look out for pupils who can tell you that multiplying or dividing the numerator and denominator by the same number will give an equivalent fraction. Pupils should be encouraged to see patterns and make generalisations at all times when appropriate.

Note

It would be beneficial to include tenths when you teach place value, because that is where it fits best, in that tenths are part of place value.

Challenge 2 Answer

Fahmida is sometimes correct. When numbers are divided by 10 the digits move one place to the right, because the value of each digit becomes 10 times smaller. But only numbers that end in 1 to 9 produce tenths; multiples of 10 do not.

Assessment

Assess the pupils' explanation of how they know that Fahmida is sometimes correct. They should write examples of numbers that produce tenths when divided by 10, and examples of numbers that don't do that. Encourage them to include both one- and two-digit numbers. Some pupils may choose to write larger numbers, which is acceptable.

Drawing place value grids would help pupils to be clear. For example:

10	1	.	$\frac{1}{10}$
6	7		
	6	.	7

10	1	.	$\frac{1}{10}$
8	0		
		8	

Can pupils make the link between $\frac{7}{10}$ and 0.7? If they can't see the equivalence between them, this would be something to work on with the whole class.

Can they read the numbers they make with both the fraction and the decimal, for example, 6.7 and $6\frac{7}{10}$?

Note

It is important to always help the pupils to make connections, and linking fractions with their decimal equivalents is an important connection. It would be helpful to do this while teaching place value, so that the pupils can see that $\frac{1}{10}$ is 10 times smaller than 1.

Challenge 3 Answer

24 can be divided into halves, thirds, quarters, sixths, eighths, twelfths and twenty-fourths.

Assessment

Assess the pupils' knowledge of fractions as they carry out the task. They should be able to tell you that the whole is 24 and that the fractions they are making are the parts. They should be able to tell you that 24 is divided into the number of parts as indicated by the denominator.

The division model for fractions is sharing. Expect them to tell you that the numerator is the number of parts being considered. Do they write number statements such as $\frac{1}{2}$ of 24 = 12, $\frac{1}{3}$ of 24 = 8, $\frac{2}{3}$ of 24 = 16? Encourage them to write all the fraction statements that they can so they have a mixture of unit and non-unit fractions. If they can do this they are showing resilience.

Can they see the link between multiplication tables and knowledge of multiplication and division facts? Finding fractions is easy if they know these facts.

Note

Using the precise vocabulary is important. They shouldn't be referring to the 'top number' and the 'bottom number' of the fraction. It should be 'numerator' and 'denominator'. The line separating them is called the 'vinculum'.

Challenge 4 Answer

The pupils should have made 2 halves, 4 quarters and 8 eighths.

The parts of one hour are 30 minutes, 15 minutes and $7\frac{1}{2}$ minutes.

The parts of one kilogram are 500g, 250g, 125g (not $\frac{1}{2}$kg, $\frac{1}{4}$kg and $\frac{1}{8}$kg).

Assessment

As pupils carry out the task, observe how they make their fraction strips and how they draw their diagram.

Do the two match? Can they tell you any equivalences? For example, $\frac{1}{2}$ is equivalent to $\frac{2}{4}$ and also to $\frac{4}{8}$, and $\frac{1}{4}$ is equivalent to $\frac{2}{8}$. Can they tell you how many halves are equivalent to one whole, and can they repeat this for quarters and eighths?

Finding the unit fractions for one hour and one kilogram are relatively simple. Assess how they do this. Halving is the obvious method, so encourage them to work on finding non-unit fractions, for example $\frac{3}{8}$ of one hour, $\frac{5}{8}$ of one kilogram. If they can do this, that shows a depth of mastery. Can they tell you that they would need to multiply by the numerator?

Do they know that 1000 grams are equivalent to one kilogram? You might need to remind them, so that they can successfully find the fractions of the kilogram in grams.

Note

Finding fractions of measurement is good practice, and should be carried out with the whole class. You could ask pupils to find fractions of lengths, capacities, volumes and money. This would involve discussing units of measure, and makes good connections with the measurement units of work required by the National Curriculum.

Number – Fractions

Fractions of shapes

Challenge 5: What fractions has this shape been divided into?

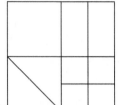

Write down each fraction and how many of each sort you can see.

Explain how you know.

What do you notice?

Challenge 6: Draw this shape on a piece of paper. Remember to include the diagonals.

Now prove that all the parts are quarters. You can cut out the parts to do this.

Fractions of numbers

Challenge 7: Look at this bar model. If the whole is 45, what is the value of one part?

What is the value of two parts? Three parts? Four parts?

If the whole is 75, what is the value of one part?

What is the value of two parts? Three parts? Four parts?

Make up your own values for the whole and then find the parts.

Challenge 8: Tom spent two-fifths of his money on a book.

If the book cost £10, how much money did he start off with?

What if the book cost £15?

What if the book cost £25?

Draw a bar model to show this problem.

Explain how you know how much money he started off with.

Make up some other amounts that the book could cost.

National Curriculum objective, Year 3, Fractions

- *recognise, find and write fractions of a discrete set of objects: unit fractions and non-unit fractions with small denominators*

Challenge 5 Answer

A quarter, four-eighths, four-sixteenths. The pupils should notice that, although some of the fractions are not the same shape as each other, they are the same area.

Assessment

Assess whether pupils can identify fractions according to the area or space they take up, and not according to the congruent shapes they see. They may not have come across sixteenths yet, but assess their ability to reason, make connections and recognise patterns; halving a whole gives a half, halving a half gives a quarter, and halving a quarter gives an eighth, so halving an eighth will give a sixteenth.

Note

If the pupils identify fractions through shape, provide opportunities for them to see fractions as different shapes, as in this question. If you don't, they are likely to develop misconceptions. It would be helpful to introduce the idea of area as the amount of space a fraction of a shape takes up.

Challenge 6 Answer

The triangles are all quarters. To prove it, you can cut each triangle in half, and these eight parts all match. Each part is now an eighth, and two-eighths make a quarter.

Assessment

Assess the pupils' ability to prove that these are all quarters. They may assume they aren't because the triangles are different shapes.

Can they fold or cut each triangle into two parts that are all identical? Can they tell you that the two parts of each triangle are eighths of the whole? Expect them to be able to tell you that two-eighths are equivalent to one-quarter, so each of those original triangles is a quarter of the whole shape.

Note

Pupils should be able to generalise that they multiply or divide the numerator and denominator by the same number to create an equivalent fraction. Give them plenty of opportunities to explore this. In the past, many teachers have tended to tell pupils the rule, but they need to apply their reasoning skills and develop the generalisation for themselves.

National Curriculum objective, Year 3, Fractions

- *recognise and use fractions as numbers: unit fractions and non-unit fractions with small denominators*

Challenge 7 Answer

45: 9, 18, 27, 36

75: 15, 30, 45, 60

Assessment

Assess whether pupils can confidently identify the parts as fifths. Expect them to be able to divide 45 by 5 using their knowledge of multiplication and division facts. Expect them then to multiply 9 by 2, 3 and 4 quickly and fluently.

Assess how they find one part of 75. Partitioning into 50 and 25 would make this simple, showing that each part is worth 15. Assess their ability to count in 15s, which would be one obvious way to find the different parts.

Encourage them to make up their own wholes and find the different parts again. What do they notice that the whole must be? Can they tell you that in order to keep the parts whole numbers it needs to be a multiple of five?

Challenge 8 Answer

£25, £37.50, £62.50

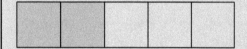

Assessment

Assess whether the pupils identify that they need five-fifths for the whole amount of money.

Assess whether they can confidently draw the model to show the problem. It is similar to the model in Challenge 7, but with two parts shaded to represent the amount Tom spent on the book.

How do they find the total? Do they halve the cost of the book and then multiply by five? How do they multiply by five? Do they use the mental calculation strategy of multiplying by 10 and halving? Do they use partitioning?

Encourage them to make up other costs for the book and work out how much money Tom started off with. Do they challenge themselves and make up amounts that involve pence as the last two values in the problem? For example £28.50.

What do they notice about the amounts? Can they tell you that they need to be multiples of two in order to find half?

Number – Fractions

Equivalent fractions

Challenge 9: Write an explanation with examples and diagrams to help Fahmida understand why we multiply or divide the numerator and denominator by the same number.

> I know that to find an equivalent fraction I have to multiply or divide the numerator and denominator by the same number. But I don't know why.

Challenge 10: Draw a bar model to show thirds.

Now draw another underneath to show sixths.

Now draw another underneath to show twelfths.

Write down all the equivalent fractions that your bars show.

Now use the generalisation to create other equivalent fractions.

Adding and subtracting fractions

Challenge 11:

1 whole								
$\frac{1}{9}$	$\frac{1}{9}$	$\frac{1}{9}$	$\frac{1}{9}$	$\frac{1}{9}$	$\frac{1}{9}$	$\frac{1}{9}$	$\frac{1}{9}$	$\frac{1}{9}$

Here is an addition that can be made using ninths:

$\frac{1}{9}$	$\frac{2}{9}$
$\frac{3}{9}$	

$\frac{1}{9} + \frac{2}{9} = \frac{3}{9}$

Because we know that, we also know that $\frac{2}{9} + \frac{1}{9} = \frac{3}{9}$, and that $\frac{3}{9} - \frac{2}{9} = \frac{1}{9}$, and also that $\frac{3}{9} - \frac{1}{9} = \frac{2}{9}$.

Make up eight other additions using ninths. Represent them using a bar model, and write the other facts you know.

Challenge 12: Write an explanation to show how Tom can add two fractions with different denominators. Use a bar model to describe your explanation.

> I can add $\frac{1}{2}$ and $\frac{1}{4}$. The sum is $\frac{3}{4}$.

Can you think of any other fractions with different denominators that you can add together?

Challenge 9 Answer

$\frac{1}{3}$			
$\frac{1}{6}$		$\frac{1}{6}$	
$\frac{1}{12}$	$\frac{1}{12}$	$\frac{1}{12}$	$\frac{1}{12}$

The diagram shows that $\frac{1}{3} = \frac{2}{6} = \frac{4}{12}$. The numerator and denominator of $\frac{1}{3}$ are multiplied by 2 for $\frac{2}{6}$ and 4 for $\frac{4}{12}$.
Accept explanations that clearly show the generalisation, with diagrams to make this obvious.

Assessment

Assess whether pupils have a deep understanding of why the numerator and denominator are multiplied or divided by the same number to create equivalent fractions.

Encourage them to draw pairs of bars to show simple equivalences such as halves and quarters, thirds and sixths, and fifths and tenths. Can they write the equivalences made? For example $\frac{1}{2} = \frac{2}{4}$; $\frac{1}{3} = \frac{2}{6}$; $\frac{2}{3} = \frac{4}{6}$; $\frac{1}{5} = \frac{2}{10}$; $\frac{2}{5} = \frac{4}{10}$; $\frac{3}{5} = \frac{6}{10}$; and $\frac{4}{5} = \frac{8}{10}$. To make each of these equivalences, the pupils simply double both the numerator and the denominator.

Ensure they include examples where they need to multiply by another number, for example $\frac{1}{3} = \frac{3}{9}$. This will show a deeper understanding. Ask them to explain to you how the generalisation is made.

Note

Making generalisations is an important reasoning skill, and regular opportunities should be given for this to happen.

Challenge 10 Answer

$\frac{1}{3} = \frac{2}{6} = \frac{4}{12}$; $\frac{2}{3} = \frac{4}{6} = \frac{8}{12}$; $\frac{3}{6} = \frac{6}{12}$; and $\frac{5}{6} = \frac{10}{12}$
Accept any other correct equivalences, for example $\frac{1}{3} = \frac{5}{15}$ and $\frac{1}{6} = \frac{3}{18}$.

Assessment

Assess how accurately pupils draw their bars. Encourage them to measure their bar using a ruler. A bar of 24cm would work well. The thirds would be 8cm, the sixths would be 4cm and the twelfths would be 2cm in width.

Can they find all the equivalent fractions on these bars? Assess how they find other equivalences. Do they take a unit fraction, for example $\frac{1}{3}$, and use their knowledge of multiples of 3 to generate more? Do they remember to multiply both the numerator and denominator by the same number, for example multiplying both by 3 to change $\frac{1}{3}$ to the equivalent $\frac{3}{9}$?

Encourage them to draw models to show clearly that the equivalent fractions they make are indeed equivalent:

$\frac{1}{3}$			$\frac{1}{3}$			$\frac{1}{3}$		
$\frac{1}{9}$	$\frac{1}{9}$	$\frac{1}{9}$	$\frac{1}{9}$	$\frac{1}{9}$	$\frac{1}{9}$	$\frac{1}{9}$	$\frac{1}{9}$	$\frac{1}{9}$

- *add and subtract fractions with the same denominator within one whole*

Challenge 11 Answer

Accept any correct examples of adding ninths, but only if models are drawn and the facts written.

Assessment

Assess the calculations that the pupils write. Ensure their bar model drawings match the calculation.

Assess their understanding of using a calculation to make commutative and inverse statements.

Note

This would be something to work on with the whole class. It is important that the pupils make connections between whole numbers and fractions where appropriate. They have looked at making two addition statements for whole numbers using the idea of commutativity, and this also works for fractions. They have looked at making inverse subtraction statements for whole numbers. Again, this also works for fractions. If we don't make links like this, many pupils believe that fractions are completely different from whole numbers and that the processes of adding and subtracting them are also different, so they think they are learning something totally new.

Challenge 12 Answer

Explanations that involve knowing that $\frac{1}{2}$ is equivalent to $\frac{2}{4}$, and so $\frac{1}{2} + \frac{1}{4}$ is equivalent to $\frac{2}{4} + \frac{1}{4}$, which equals $\frac{3}{4}$, are acceptable, as long as a bar model is also used to show this.

Assessment

Assess how confidently the pupils write their explanation and draw the bar model to represent what they are thinking.

The National Curriculum requirements do not state that pupils need to add and subtract fractions with different denominators. However, they have explored halves and quarters throughout Key Stage 1, and so should have been adding and subtracting them through the models and representations that they have used.

This is a reasoning task to show you whether the pupils can say why this happens. You could also ask them to write down what else they know, if they already know that $\frac{1}{2} + \frac{1}{4} = \frac{3}{4}$ ($\frac{1}{4} + \frac{1}{2} = \frac{3}{4}$, $\frac{3}{4} - \frac{1}{2} = \frac{1}{4}$, $\frac{3}{4} - \frac{1}{4} = \frac{1}{2}$).

Assess the other addition examples the pupils make up. Do these examples relate to the equivalent fractions they have practised making?

Number – Fractions

Comparing and ordering fractions

Challenge 13:

I think $\frac{1}{2}$ is smaller than $\frac{1}{5}$ because 2 is less than 5.

Do you agree with Tom?

Explain your reasoning in words and diagrams.

Write down pairs of unit fractions, and compare them using > and <.

Challenge 14: Do you agree with Fahmida?

Write an explanation to show how to do this for someone who does not know.

I can order fractions with the same denominator in increasing and also decreasing order. It's really easy.

Give different examples to show how you can order fractions.

Solving problems

Challenge 15:

I made some biscuits. I packed $\frac{2}{3}$ of them into a container and gave $\frac{1}{5}$ of what was left to Tom. I then had 40 left.

How many biscuits did Fahmida bake?

Explain how you worked this out, using a bar model.

Challenge 16:

I counted my marbles. I gave $\frac{1}{4}$ of them to my brother and $\frac{1}{3}$ of what was left to a friend. I put $\frac{1}{2}$ of the rest away and then played with the remaining 36.

How many marbles did Tom start off with?

Explain how you worked this out, using a bar model.

Challenge 13 Answer

Tom is incorrect; $\frac{1}{2}$ is greater than $\frac{1}{5}$ (as long as the whole is the same).

Assessment

Assess the pupils' explanations. They need to make the point that the denominator shows how much the whole is divided into; for halves, the whole is divided into two, and for fifths the whole is divided into five parts. If the whole is the same size, the parts showing the halves will be larger than those showing fifths. Pupils should draw two bar models the same size, and demonstrate halves and fifths on these. Encourage them to measure to make accurate models.

Can the pupils tell you that halves are not always greater than fifths? It depends on the whole. Can they give examples of when this could be? For example, $\frac{1}{2}$ of 50p is smaller than $\frac{1}{5}$ of £2.50.

Could they make up their own unit fractions, and compare them using the greater than and less than symbols?

Challenge 14 Answer

Fahmida is correct; ordering fractions with the same denominator is simple. The numerators are the numbers that need ordering.

Assessment

Assess the pupils' explanations. Do they explain that, because the denominators are the same, the numerators need to be ordered? This is because the parts are the same size. $\frac{1}{7}$ is smaller than $\frac{2}{7}$ because $\frac{1}{7}$ is just one of the same-sized parts and $\frac{2}{7}$ is two of the same-sized parts.

Did the pupils write down a selection of fractions with the same denominator in the correct order? Can they write them in both ascending and descending order?

Note

Ordering fractions with the same denominator appears very easy, but it does depend on a good understanding of basic fractions. Take time exploring these with the class, and don't rush on too quickly.

National Curriculum objective, Year 3, Fractions

- *solve problems that involve all other fractions requirements*

Challenge 15 Answer

Fahmida baked 150 biscuits.

Assessment

Assess the pupils' use of the bar model to help them make sense of this problem. Did they begin by drawing a bar and dividing it into three parts to represent thirds?

$\frac{1}{3}$	$\frac{1}{3}$	$\frac{1}{3}$

They should have shaded two of the thirds to represent the amount that Fahmida put into a container. Did they then divide the remaining third into fifths and shade one of those to show how much she gave to Tom?

$\frac{1}{3}$	$\frac{1}{3}$					

Can they identify that the four remaining parts together are 40 and therefore one part is 10? From this, they can then find that each third is worth 50, and three of these are 150.

You could add variation to this task by asking how many biscuits Fahmida baked if she had 48 / 72 / 96 / 136 biscuits left.

Note

If pupils can use the bar model confidently, we can give them more challenging problems than we have previously.

Challenge 16 Answer

Tom had 144 marbles to begin with.

Assessment

Assess the pupils' use of the bar model to help them make sense of this problem. Did they begin by drawing a bar and dividing it into four parts to represent quarters?

$\frac{1}{4}$	$\frac{1}{4}$	$\frac{1}{4}$	$\frac{1}{4}$

Did they shade one quarter to represent the amount that Tom gave his brother? Assess if pupils can identify that, after doing that, one-third of what is left is the same as a quarter of the whole bar. Did they shade this?

$\frac{1}{4}$	$\frac{1}{4}$	$\frac{1}{4}$	$\frac{1}{4}$

Can they identify that half of what is left now is also one quarter of the original whole bar? Assess whether pupils can identify that the remaining quarter is 36 and that to find the number of marbles Tom started with, we need to multiply 36 by four. How do they work this out? Doubling twice is a good mental calculation strategy to use. Pupils could partition 36 into 30 and 6, then double 30 twice to give 120, and double 6 twice to give 24. They finally recombine the two parts to give 144.

You could add variation by asking how many marbles Tom had to start with if he had 48 / 66 / 126 marbles left.

Note

If Year 3 pupils can use the bar model confidently, you could give them some of the old Level 5 fraction problems from the Year 6 SATs tests. It might be worth trying some out.

Measurement

Units of length

Challenge 1: Do you agree with Fahmida?

Explain your reasoning.

Draw three lines. Measure them in centimetres and millimetres. Find their total length. Find the difference between pairs of them.

I have three pieces of ribbon. One is 24cm and 8mm long. The second is 26cm and 7mm long, and the third is 38cm and 4mm long. In total I have 88 centimetres of ribbon.

Challenge 2: Do you agree with Tom?

Explain your reasoning.

Measure the heights of three friends in metres and centimetres. Find their total height. Find the difference between pairs of them.

My dad is 1m and 87cm tall. My mum is 1m and 63cm tall and I am 1m and 22cm tall. That means our total height is 4m and 72cm.

Units of mass

Challenge 3: Do you think Fahmida knows hundreds and hundreds of other facts?

Explain your reasoning.

Give 20 examples of other facts that you know based on what Fahmida knows. Now find the total of all your new quantities!

I know that one kilogram is equivalent to 1000g. Because I know this, I know hundreds and hundreds of other facts.

Challenge 4: Do you agree with Tom?

Explain your reasoning.

Use a set of weighing scales and find the mass of three different items from your classroom. Find their total mass. Find the difference between pairs of them.

I used a set of weighing scales to find the mass of a bag of potatoes. The pointer on the scales was halfway between 3kg and 4kg. So my bag of potatoes had a mass of 3 kilograms and 50 grams.

- *measure, compare, add and subtract: lengths (m/cm/mm); mass (kg/g); volume/capacity (L/mL)*

Challenge 1 Answer

Fahmida is incorrect. She has just added the centimetres and ignored the millimetres.
The total length is 89cm and 9mm.

Assessment

Assess the pupils' knowledge of reading centimetre and millimetre measurements. Do they know that, for example, 24cm 8mm is 24.8cm? Can they explain that 8mm is eight-tenths of a centimetre because there are 10 millimetres in a centimetre? If not, you may need to spend more time looking at the different ways to write centimetre and millimetre lengths; for example 26.7cm can be represented as 26cm 7mm or 267mm.

Can pupils explain that Fahmida has missed the millimetres? Observe how they add to find the total length. Do they use a mental calculation strategy such as sequencing, or do they perform a formal written method? If they have done the latter, ask them to check using another method. Do they realise that they simply need to add the missing millimetres to Fahmida's total?

Can they accurately draw and measure lines in centimetres and millimetres, and represent each in centimetres? Can they accurately find the total of the three? Can they find all possible differences between them (lines 1 and 2, lines 1 and 3, and lines 2 and 3)?

Note

Bringing measurement into place value is a great way to practise and make links to whole numbers and tenths. It is also helpful to bring measurement into addition and subtraction. It helps the pupils to understand that the processes of addition and subtraction are the same when working with numbers and any type of measurement.

Challenge 2 Answer

Tom is correct.

Assessment

Assess the pupils' knowledge of reading metre and centimetre measurements. Do they know that, for example, 1m 87cm is 1.87m? Can they explain that 87cm is $\frac{87}{100}$ of a metre because there are 100 centimetres in a metre? If not, you may need to spend more time looking at the different ways to write metre and centimetre lengths; for example 1m 22cm can be represented as 122cm and 1.22m. Can any pupils tell you how many millimetres are equivalent to this length?

Observe how the pupils add to find the total height in order to check that Tom is correct. Do they use a mental calculation strategy such as knowing number pairs to 10 and sequencing or bridging 10? Do they perform a formal written method? Encourage mental calculation strategies. If they have performed a written method, ask them to check using another method.

Can they accurately measure the heights of three friends in metres and centimetres, and represent this in metres? Can they accurately find the total of the three? Can they find all possible differences between them (heights 1 and 2, 1 and 3, and 2 and 3)?

Note

As mentioned in the note to Challenge 1, it is valuable to link measurement to place value. Metre measurements connect well to hundredths. Also bring this concept into addition and subtraction as part of everyday practice.

This is not a requirement of the National Curriculum for number and place value, but it is relevant.

National Curriculum objective, Year 3, Measurement

- *measure, compare, add and subtract: lengths (m/cm/mm); mass (kg/g); volume/capacity (L/mL)*

Challenge 3 Answer

Fahmida is correct. She can work out thousands of facts.

Examples from the pupils will vary.

Assessment

Assess the pupils' ability to use a known fact to generate related facts. Can they double and halve? For example, 1kg = 1000g, 2kg = 2000g, 4kg = 4000g, $\frac{1}{2}$kg = 500g, $\frac{1}{4}$kg = 250g, $\frac{1}{8}$kg = 125g. Can they use these to make other examples by addition and subtraction? For example, $2\frac{1}{4}$kg = 2250g, $4\frac{1}{2}$kg = 4500g, $1\frac{1}{8}$kg = 1125g.

Can the pupils use their knowledge of fractions to find fifths and tenths of different kilograms, for example, $\frac{1}{5}$kg = 200g, $3\frac{2}{5}$kg = 3400g, $\frac{1}{10}$kg = 100g, $4\frac{7}{10}$kg = 4700g?

To show a depth of mastery it is important that the pupils show flexibility. Some will continually use doubling when they should be thinking about other ways to make more facts. So assess the perseverance of the pupils to make 20 new facts in a variety of ways. How do they find the total of the 20 facts they made? Do they use mental calculation strategies, for example, sequencing? Do they keep a running total, using jottings as they add? If they don't, this would be a valuable method to teach for adding several numbers.

Note

Bringing measurement into addition and subtraction helps the pupils to understand that the processes of addition and subtraction are the same when working with numbers and any type of measurement.

Challenge 4 Answer

Tom is incorrect; the mass is 3kg and 500g.

Examples of the pupils' own masses will vary.

Assessment

Assess the pupils' knowledge of the units of mass. Do they know that one kilogram is equivalent to 1000g and therefore $\frac{1}{2}$kg is equivalent to 500g? Can they tell you that if the pointer on a set of scales is halfway between two kilogram intervals, that is 500g? Do they explain that Tom seems to think that 100 grams are equivalent to one kilogram, which is incorrect? The mass of his potatoes must be 3 kilograms and 500 grams.

Observe the pupils as they weigh three items from the classroom. Do they understand how to read the scale? Can they identify the value of the divisions and work out how many grams are in different positions? Can they find their mass accurately in kilograms and grams?

Can they record using only kilograms? This could involve three decimal places. If they have had experience of recording lengths in this way (3.6cm, 2.75m) they may be able to make the connection which will show a depth of understanding. If any pupils struggle to read the scales, this area of the curriculum will need some whole-class teaching sequences.

Note

Bringing measurement into addition and subtraction helps the pupils to understand that the processes of addition and subtraction are the same when with working numbers and any type of measurement.

Measurement

Units of capacity and volume

Challenge 5: Who do you think is correct?

Explain your reasoning.

Give five examples of things that would have their capacity measured in litres. Explain how you know.

Give five examples of things that would have their capacity measured in millilitres. Explain how you know.

I think that you would measure the capacity of a bath in litres.

I think you would measure its capacity in millilitres because millilitre means a million litres.

Challenge 6: Do you agree with Tom?

Explain your reasoning.

Find a measuring jug, some water and a bottle. Pour some water into the bottle. Don't fill it! Find the volume of water that is in your bottle. Do this again, making a different volume in the bottle.

I think 'volume' and 'capacity' are two words for the same measurement.

Perimeter

Challenge 7: Is what Fahmida has said sometimes, always or never true?

Explain your reasoning.

Use a ruler to draw some shapes to prove what you think.

To find the perimeter of a shape you multiply the lengths of the sides by 4 if it's a rectangle, by 5 if it's a pentagon, by 6 if it's a hexagon and so on.

Challenge 8:

I measured the perimeter of a rectangle. Its perimeter was 36cm. What do you think its width and length are?

Can you answer Tom's question?

Explain your reasoning.

Use a ruler and draw all the possible whole-centimetre rectangles.

National Curriculum objective, Year 3, Measurement

- *measure, compare, add and subtract: lengths (m/cm/mm); mass (kg/g); volume/capacity (L/mL)*

Challenge 5 Answer

Fahmida is correct.

Examples from the pupils will vary.

Assessment

Assess the pupils' understanding of 'capacity'. Can they tell you that capacity is the amount a container will hold?

Can they tell you the units that are used to measure capacity? Some pupils may tell you pints and gallons. If they do, have a conversation about these being imperial measurements that we used to use to measure capacity. The US still uses these. The UK now mostly uses metric measurement, and litres and millilitres are the units used for capacity.

Can they tell you that 1000mL is equivalent to 1 litre? This means that Tom is incorrect, a millilitre is one thousandth of a litre not one million litres. Can they tell you that a millilitre is a small unit and therefore you wouldn't measure a bath's capacity in this? Litres are used for larger containers, so a bath's capacity would be measured in litres; therefore Fahmida is correct. If at any point the pupils show a lack of understanding, build in some practical measuring lessons so that they can develop their understanding of capacity.

Can they think of five things that would have their capacity measured in litres and then another five in millilitres?

Note

Build word problem solving activities into addition and subtraction; for example, Tom's bottle had a capacity of 1.5L and Fahmida's bottle had a capacity of 750mL. What is the total capacity of both bottles? How much more capacity does Tom's bottle have?

Challenge 6 Answer

Tom is incorrect. Capacity and volume are not the same.

Assessment

Assess the pupils' understanding of 'volume' and 'capacity'. Can they tell you that volume is the amount in a container at a given time, and capacity is the amount a container can hold?

Can they tell you the units that are used to measure volume? Are they aware that the same units are used to measure capacity?

Ask them to tell you how many millilitres are equivalent to 1 litre and then $\frac{1}{2}$ litre, $\frac{1}{4}$ litre and $\frac{1}{8}$ litre. Can they use halving efficiently to do this? If not, you might need to do some starter activities around doubling and halving. Give the pupils a bottle or a glass half filled with water, and ask them to describe the volume (the amount of water in the bottle or glass at the moment) and capacity (how much the bottle or glass will hold). Can they tell you that the bottle or glass is not filled to its capacity?

Observe the pupils as they carry out their task. How full do they fill their bottle? Can they then pour the water into a measuring jug and read the scale accurately in litres and millilitres, if appropriate, or just millilitres?

Note

Build word problem activities into addition and subtraction, for example: The capacity of Fahmida's bottle is 2L. So is Tom's. They were full of water at the beginning of the day. By lunchtime Fahmida's bottle contained a volume of 1L 200mL. Tom's bottle had a volume of 500mL. What is the total volume of water that they have both drunk?

National Curriculum objective, Year 3, Measurement

- *measure the perimeter of simple 2-D shapes*

Challenge 7 Answer

What Fahmida said is sometimes true. Examples from the pupils will vary.

Assessment

Assess the pupils' understanding of 'perimeter'. Can they tell you that the perimeter is the distance around an area? Look out for pupils who don't just relate perimeter to particular shapes, but understand that every space has a perimeter. Ask them to give examples, such as the outside edges of the classroom floor, a table, a field. If they can do this, they are showing a greater depth of mastery of perimeter.

Can they verbally explain why what Fahmida says is sometimes true, as well as explaining it in writing? Do their drawn examples match what they have written?

They should be able to work out that the statement is true for regular shapes, for example, if the sides of a square measure 8cm, then this would be multiplied by four to give a perimeter of 32cm; if the sides of a regular pentagon measure 10cm, then this would be multiplied by 5 to give a perimeter of 50cm. But to find the perimeter of irregular shapes, all the sides would need measuring and adding, or if some lengths are the same, a mixture of addition and multiplication.

Note

You could use perimeter as part of practice activities for addition and subtraction, and also as part of geometry lessons. When talking about properties of 2-D shapes, discuss sides, corners and their angles, and lines of symmetry, and ask the pupils to find their perimeters. This would develop a deeper understanding of this concept than if you only covered it during measurement for one or two days.

Challenge 8 Answer

Possible widths and lengths using whole centimetres are: 1cm × 17cm, 2cm × 16cm, 3cm × 15cm, 4cm × 14cm, 5cm × 13cm, 6cm × 12cm, 7cm × 11cm, 8cm × 10cm, and 9cm × 9cm.

Assessment

Assess the pupils' ability to be systematic in their approach to this problem. A valuable area of mathematical thinking is working systematically. Pupils need to be shown how to do this, as they often approach this sort of problem in a random way and can't keep track of what they are doing. It is also easier to spot patterns when working systematically.

Do they start with a side of 1cm, realise that two of the sides must be 1cm and take 2 from 36 and then notice that the other two sides total 34cm, so halve this to give 17cm? They then should work with two sides of 2cm and use a similar approach to find the other two sides.

How quickly do they notice a pattern? If they spot the pattern quickly, they are working at greater depth. Observe how they draw all the shapes. Are they accurate when they measure? What do they notice about the 9cm × 9cm rectangle? Ask them if these are the only possible shapes. Can they tell you that many more can be made if using centimetres and millimetres? Ask them to give you a few examples, such as 1.5cm × 16.5cm and 2.5cm × 15.5cm. Do they notice that there is a pattern again?

Note

As noted in Challenge 7, it would be valuable to use perimeter as part of practice activities for addition and subtraction, and also as part of geometry lessons.

Measurement

Money

Challenge 9: I bought a sandwich at the café. I paid with three £1 coins and received one coin in change.

How much could Tom's sandwich have cost?

Explain your reasoning.

Find all the possibilities.

Challenge 10: Do you agree with Fahmida?

Explain your reasoning.

Write down six different ways to make £3.50.

 I can make £3.50 using two coins.

Telling the time

Challenge 11: I can work out the Roman numerals from 1 to 12 by comparing these analogue clock faces.

Is Fahmida correct? Explain your reasoning.

Write down the Roman numerals from 1 to 12, and beside them write the equivalent numbers in our number system.

Challenge 12: Use these digits to make up as many 24-hour clock times as you can.

0   1   2   3

Draw your times as analogue clocks, and label them using analogue labels.

Challenge 9 Answer

It depends on the coin Tom received in change:

- If he'd received a 50p coin, it would have cost £2.50;
- If he'd received a 20p coin, it would have cost 2.80;
- If he'd received a 10p coin, it would have cost £2.90;
- If he'd received a 5p coin, it would have cost £2.95;
- If he'd received a 2p coin it would have cost £2.98;
- If he'd received a 1p coin it would have cost £2.99.

If pupils have given a £2 coin or £1 coin as the answer, discuss how these are not realistic solutions as they indicate that Tom handed over three £1 coins unnecessarily.

Assessment

Assess the pupils' understanding of money. Find out if they know all the coins and notes in our monetary system, and their values in numbers of pence. Ask them to tell you different ways to make different values using the least number of coins, for example, 67p (50p, 10p, 5p, 2p). If they have not mastered this, then spend some time with the whole class on money.

Observe how they tackle the problem. Do they do this systematically? If they don't, they are likely to miss some possibilities. It might be that you need to spend time helping pupils develop this skill.

Note

You could use money as part of practice activities for place value; 1p, 10p and £1 coins are great for this. Once the pupils have shown, for example, 465 using money (£4.65) they could then work out how to make this amount using the fewest number of coins (£2, £2, 50p, 10p, 5p).

Also use money as part of practice activities for addition and subtraction. Most pupils will need lots of practice with this concept, and covering it during measurement alone might not be enough time to develop mastery.

Challenge 10 Answer

Fahmida is incorrect; she cannot make £3.50 using two coins.

Assessment

Ask the pupils why Fahmida might think she can make £3.50 using two coins; for example, she may think that there is a £3 coin. Assess the pupils as they carry out the task, again looking for the fewest possible coins to give as part of their explanation. Fahmida could use three coins, £2, £1 and 50p.

Assess the other suggestions made for making £3.50. Encourage sensible ideas that use a variety of coins – for example, £2, £1, 20p, 20p and 10p – this will enable you to assess how much they really know about money.

Note

Some pupils find the concept of money difficult. Many don't have the opportunity to use it, and don't see parents or carers using it because people often pay with cards these days.

An important aspect of teaching about money is to give the pupils a feel for the value of money. This is a life skill that pupils need to learn. Giving them the opportunity to use money in practice activities for place value and the four operations will mean that they develop a better understanding.

National Curriculum objective, Year 3, Measurement

- **tell and write the time from an analogue clock, including using Roman numerals from I to XII, and 12-hour and 24-hour clocks**
- **use vocabulary such as o'clock, a.m./p.m., morning, afternoon, noon and midnight**

Challenge 11 Answer

Fahmida is correct.

Assessment

Assess the pupils' understanding of Roman numerals by observing if they link the hour numbers in our number system with the Roman numerals for the same hours. Assess their lists to see if the two types of number match: I and 1, II and 2, III and 3, IV and 4, V and 5, VI and 6, VII and 7, VIII and 8, IX and 9, X and 10, XI and 11, and XII and 12.

Ask them to think of a reason why IV is 4 and VI, VII and VIII are 6, 7 and 8. Ask them to think why IX is 9 and XI and XII are 11 and 12.

Can they tell you that IV is one before 5 and therefore 4, VI is one after 5, VII is 2 after 5 and VIII is 3 after 5? Can they tell you that IX is one before 10 and XI and XII are one and two after 10?

You could ask them to write the other numbers to 30 following this pattern. If they can do that, they are showing depth of understanding of how to use pattern.

Note

If you carry out a topic on the Romans, then Roman numerals and clocks with Roman numerals are an obvious area to cover.

Challenge 12 Answer

01:23, 01:32, 02:13, 02:31, 03:12, 03:21, 10:23, 10:32, 12:03, 12:30, 13:02, 13:20, 20:13, 20:31, 21:03, 21:30, 23:01, 23:10,

Assessment

Assess the pupils' understanding of 24-hour clock time before they begin the task. Do they understand that from 12 noon the hour numbers continue to increase rather than going back to 1? Find out if they know where 24-hour clock time is often used; for example, bus timetables, phones, computers.

Assess how they carried out the task. Were they being systematic? If they weren't they may have missed some times.

Did they really think about the times, and realise that they cannot make times that have a three in the tens position for the hours, for example, 30:12, because the hours can be no greater than 23?

Do their analogue clocks match the digital times? And are they labelled correctly? For example, 23 minutes past 1 a.m. If they haven't added a.m. and p.m., ask how they can make it clear that they have drawn a morning or afternoon/evening time. They should add these to their analogue labels.

If any pupils have, for example, written 31 minutes past 2, ask them if they can think of another way to write it (29 minutes to 3).

If they can do all of the above, they have really mastered telling the time.

Note

The expectations for time in the National Curriculum are set high. It would be a good idea to regularly revisit this, maybe during starter activities.

Measurement

Comparing times

Challenge 13:

It took Fahmida 1 hour and 55 minutes to complete her homework. She started at 4:35, so must have finished at 5:90.

Is Tom correct?

Explain your reasoning.

Challenge 14:

Within a single day, 23 minutes past 11 is a later time than 14 minutes past 10.

Is Fahmida's statement sometimes, always or never true?

Write the two times in eight different digital ways.

Units of time

Challenge 15:

I know that 60 seconds are equivalent to one minute. Because I know this, I know hundreds of other facts.

Tom is correct!

Explain your reasoning. Make up interesting examples to prove Tom is correct.

Challenge 16:

Someone told me that there are common years and leap years. I don't really understand. Life is made up of lots of years, so they must all be common.

Can you help Fahmida understand what these different years are?

Explain, with examples.

National Curriculum objective, Year 3, Measurement

- *estimate and read time with increasing accuracy to the nearest minute; record and compare times in terms of seconds, minutes and hours*

Challenge 13 Answer

Tom is incorrect. She finishes at 6.30.

Assessment

Assess the pupils' understanding of the units we use to measure time. Do they know that 60 seconds are equivalent to one minute and that 60 minutes are equivalent to one hour? Are they aware that time is base 60 and our number system is base 10? This means we cannot add times in the same way that we would add numbers.

What do the pupils think that Tom has done wrong to give the time of 5:90? Can they explain that he has just added the minutes together as we would ordinary numbers?

Do the pupils know that the exchange happens at 60 to give one hour and any left will be minutes? So Tom should have added the minutes, exchanged 60 of them for an hour, added that to the hours number and made the time 6:30.

If the pupils can explain all this they are showing an even greater depth of mastery in the concept of time. Give other similar problems for them to solve: keep the context and starting time the same, but change the number of minutes that Fahmida spends on her homework. Ensure the times in the answer will need a change to the hours.

Note

You could set problems like these as practice activities when you are teaching addition and subtraction for confident pupils. This will give them the experience of moving between different bases.

Challenge 14 Answer

Fahmida's statement is sometimes true.

11:23 a.m., 11:23 p.m. 10:14 a.m., 10:14 p.m., 11:23, 23:23, 10:14, 22:14

Assessment

Assess the pupils' understanding of telling the time accurately to the nearest minute. You could give them clocks and ask them to show you different times. You could say the times in a mixture of analogue, 12-hour and 24-hour times. Can the pupils show them accurately? If not, you probably need to work on time with the class so that the pupils can begin to develop mastery in this area of mathematics.

Ask the pupils to first explain why Fahmida is correct; if both the times are morning times, 10 o'clock comes before 11 o'clock so 23 minutes past 11 is later than 14 minutes past 10. It is the same if both times are in the evening. Can they think of a time that shows Fahmida is not correct? 23 minutes past 11 in the morning is not later than 14 minutes past 10 in the evening. Assess how clearly they write about this.

Can the pupils write the two times as both 12-hour and 24-hour times? If they can explain that Fahmida's statement is sometimes true, with proof to show why she is correct and why she is incorrect, and if they can record these times in eight different digital ways, they are evidencing mastery in this aspect of the curriculum.

Challenge 15 Answer

Tom is correct.

Assessment

Assess the pupils' understanding of the units we use to measure time. Do they know that 60 seconds are equivalent to a minute? Before they carry out the task, ask them how they can use this fact to generate other facts.

Encourage them to think about the other numerical skills that they have learnt, for example doubling and halving, multiplying and dividing by 10, and also addition and subtraction. When they carry out the task, look for examples such as 120 seconds = 2 minutes, 1200 seconds = 20 minutes, 30 seconds = $\frac{1}{2}$ minute, 15 seconds = $\frac{1}{4}$ minute, 1320 seconds = 22 minutes. Look out for those pupils who can convert to hours as well, for example, 12 000 seconds = 200 minutes = 3 hours 20 minutes.

If the pupils can confidently create new facts, they are working at a depth of mastery. If they can't, teach some sessions on using what you already know to create new facts. This will help the pupils become flexible thinkers.

Note

This type of activity can be included in work on multiplication and division as a practice activity to help the pupils see the practical application of what they learn.

Challenge 16 Answer

Answers depend on children's explanations.

Assessment

Before the pupils carry out the task, assess their understanding of leap years and common years. Do they know that a common year has 365 days and a leap year has 366? Some may be familiar with these if they have friends or family members who were born in a leap year.

Can they tell you that a leap year is a calendar year containing one additional day added to keep the calendar year in line with the seasonal year? Seasons do not repeat in a whole number of days, so if the years always have the same number of days there will be a drift over time. By adding an extra day into the fourth year, this drift can be corrected. All other years are referred to as common years. You may have to teach the pupils this before they carry out the task.

Can they tell you that 2016 was a leap year? If not, tell them that it was. Can they work out from that information that leap years are multiples of four?

They should now be able to successfully explain the difference to Fahmida and show examples of leap years that are multiples of four, for example, 2000, 2004, 2008 and 2012. Can they tell you any leap years from last century, for example, 1984, 1988, 1992 and 1996?

Measurement

Time durations

Challenge 17:

I went for a bike ride. I left home at 14:25 and got back home at 15:13.

I went for a bike ride too. I left home at 20 past 2 and got back at 5 minutes past 3.

Who went out for the longer bike ride?

Explain your reasoning.

Challenge 18:

There was a sale at the toy shop near where I live. It started on 24 February and ended on 20 March.

For how many days did the sale last?

Explain your reasoning.

National Curriculum objective, Year 3, Measurement

- *compare durations of events [for example to calculate the time taken by particular events or tasks]*

Challenge 17 Answer

Tom went on the longer bike ride. His was 48 minutes. Fahmida's ride lasted 45 minutes.

Assessment

This is the first time the National Curriculum has required year 3 pupils to find time durations.

Before pupils begin the task, assess their understanding of finding time durations. How do they do this? Do they use time number lines or another method? If they don't yet have a method, you could teach them to use time number lines. Ask them to find the duration from one time to another, for example 7:18 to 8:40, and model this method:

+42 mins   +40 mins

7:18   8:00   8:40

42 mins + 40 mins = 82 mins = 1 hour 22 minutes

Observe how they carry out the task. Do they use time number lines to find the durations of the bike rides?

+35 mins +13 mins

14:25   15:00 15:13

35 mins + 13 mins = 48 minutes

Any method is acceptable as long as the pupils find the correct solution. Ensure it is efficient. Can they move between analogue and digital times with ease? If not, this would be something to work on during class mathematics lessons.

Note

Ensure the pupils don't confuse time number lines, which are in base 60, with the number lines that they usually use for number work, which are in base 10.

Challenge 18 Answer

As no year is specified, there could be two answers: 25 days if a common year or 26 days if a leap year. Ensure pupils include the start date in their count.

Assessment

Before pupils answer the problem, ask them what they know about common years and leap years. What is the difference? Why do we have leap years? (Refer to Challenge 16.) Discuss how this might impact on the answer to the problem. You could provide a calendar page for a year to aid the pupils or you might prefer them to use a counting on strategy and draw a date number line, for example:

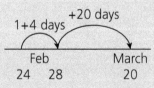

1+4 days   +20 days

Feb   March
24   28   20

Assess whether they notice that the sale begins in February, which could have 28 or 29 days. Expect pupils to give you the answer for both a common year and for a leap year.

Note

Calendars are a great resource for rehearsing mental calculation strategies. For example, ask the pupils to start on a certain date and move on 14 days. The quickest way to do this would be to convert the days to an equivalent number of weeks, thus practising multiplication facts for seven. You could ask them to add on 24/48/72/96 hours. The pupils would need to find the equivalent number of days for the given hours.

Geometry – Properties of shapes

2–D and 3–D shapes

Challenge 1:

 I wonder what polyhedra these could be the faces of?

Help Tom out. Think of all the 3-D shapes that have faces the same as these 2-D shapes. Sketch the 3-D shapes. Label them with the correct names.

Challenge 2:

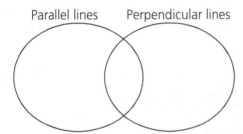

 I wonder what 2-D shapes I could fit into my Venn diagram?

Can you help Fahmida? Draw a Venn diagram like Fahmida's, but larger. Draw four shapes in each section, and label them with their names.

Angles

Challenge 3:

 My teacher said that angles are a property of a shape and also a direction of a turn. I wonder what she means?

Use the pictures to help Tom understand what is meant by 'angles are a property of shape' and 'a direction of turn'. Explain your reasoning clearly.

Challenge 4:

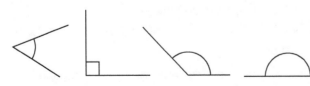 I found these diagrams in my brother's maths book. I wonder what they are?

Can you help Fahmida? Write down everything you know about each diagram.

National Curriculum objectives, Year 3, Geometry

- *draw 2-D shapes and make 3-D shapes using modelling materials; recognise 3-D shapes in different orientations and describe them*
- *identify horizontal and vertical lines and pairs of perpendicular and parallel lines*

Challenge 1 Answer

- The square could be the face of a cube, cuboid or square-based pyramid.
- The rectangle could be the face of a cuboid or any type of prism.
- The triangle could be the face of a triangular prism or any type of pyramid.
- The hexagon could be the face of a hexagonal-based pyramid or a hexagonal prism.
- The pentagon could be the face of a pentagonal-based pyramid or a pentagonal prism.

Assessment

Assess whether the pupils know that 3-D shapes with faces and not curved surfaces are polyhedra. This might be new vocabulary for them. Assess whether they can identify the 2-D shapes that Tom is talking about. Do any of them say that the square is a diamond? If they do, correct that misconception; it has four sides the same length and four right angles, so it is a square that is simply in a different orientation.

Pupils should be able to identify all five shapes. Can they tell you that the triangle is equilateral because all its sides and angles are the same? This is not a requirement for Year 3, but it is worth sharing. Introducing vocabulary as it arises is good practice.

Before pupils carry out the task, show a variety of 3-D shapes and ask them to name them and talk about their properties in terms of faces, edges, vertices and the shape names of their faces. Do they know that, apart from the regular polyhedra, 3-D polyhedra are either pyramids or prisms? There are five regular polyhedra, and pupils should know cube and tetrahedron. Do the pupils write about octahedron and icosahedron (20 faces) for triangular faces and dodecahedron for pentagon? This isn't expected yet. They need to know that spheres, hemispheres, cones and cylinders all have one or more curved surfaces and are not polyhedra.

Observe the pupils as they work. Can they identify all possible 3-D shapes? Can they sketch them with some accuracy? Do they label them with the correct name?

Challenge 2 Answer

There are many possible 2-D shapes. Ensure pupils match the properties for parallel and perpendicular sides. Pupils should include square and oblong in the intersection – and perhaps some irregular shapes with one pair of each.

Assessment

Do pupils know what parallel and perpendicular lines are? Can they identify them in the classroom? It is important that they understand that parallel lines never meet, and that perpendicular lines form right angles which can be in different orientations. They should be able to tell you that rectangles and parallelograms are the only quadrilaterals with two pairs of parallel and perpendicular sides. Ask them to draw two irregular shapes that may have only one pair of each. Can they tell you that rectangles are four-sided shapes with four right angles? Can they also tell you that a regular rectangle is a square and an irregular one is an oblong?

During this task, encourage them to draw appropriate regular and irregular shapes in each section. Part of their task is to label each shape. Encourage the pupils to be accurate with their labelling.

Note

Precise mathematical vocabulary should be introduced as it arises. Therefore it might be appropriate to introduce polyhedron, polyhedral, equilateral triangle, trapezium, parallelogram and other named four-sided shapes.

National Curriculum objectives, Year 3, Geometry

- *recognise angles as a property of a shape or a direction of a turn*
- *identify right angles; recognise that two right angles makes a half-turn, three make three-quarters of a turn and four a complete turn; identify whether angles are greater than or less than a right angle*
- *identify horizontal and vertical lines and pairs of perpendicular and parallel lines*

Challenge 3 Answer

Various answers are likely to be given. Ensure these include ones meaning that the corners of 2-D shapes form angles as a property of shape; and that movements to, for example, left and right, or clockwise and anticlockwise, are angles as a direction of turn.

Assessment

Before the pupils carry out the task, assess their current knowledge of angles. Do they recognise that the corners of a shape give an angle which is the distance from one side of the shape to the next one? They should know that a square has four right angles and that these are a quarter of a turn.

They should know that a corner of a pentagon is also a turn from one side to another. Regular pentagons have five angles that are greater than a right angle. But the pentagon pictured is irregular; it has two angles that are a quarter-turn because they are right angles, two greater than a quarter-turn, and one that is less. The pupils should use all this information to explain angles as a property of a shape to Tom.

Do they also know that angles are a direction of turn? Are they familiar with clockwise and anticlockwise turns that can be described in the fractional sizes of quarter, half and three-quarters? They learnt about these in Year 2, so should be able to tell you this. If they have forgotten, it would be a good idea to remind them before they complete the task.

Ask them to use and develop this to explain angles as a direction of turn. They should describe the road signs in these terms. For example, the first sign indicates a roundabout and shows a complete anticlockwise turn. The second shows a quarter-turn to the left or in an anticlockwise direction.

Note

Due to time constraints and the volume of requirements in the National Curriculum, this area of shape often has less time spent on it and may not be fully mastered. So it is important to check the pupils' understanding of the Year 2 requirements before teaching those for Year 3.

Challenge 4 Answer

Various answers are likely to be given. Ensure that the pupils write about the size of the turns from one line to the other.

Assessment

Before the pupils carry out the task, assess their current knowledge of the size of angles. They have previously explored these using the vocabulary of quarter, half and three-quarter turns. They should know that a quarter-turn is a right angle.

Assess their descriptions of the diagrams. Do they talk about the first diagram being smaller than a right angle? If they have described this as an acute angle, accept that, because it is correct although this term is not officially taught until Year 4.

They should write about the second angle being a right angle, which is a quarter-turn. They should write about the third angle being greater than a right angle but less than a straight line angle. If they use the term 'obtuse', accept this because it is the correct vocabulary although again, they aren't introduced to this until Year 4.

The fourth diagram shows a straight line angle, which is equivalent to two quarter-turns, which is equivalent to a half-turn. The final angle shows a complete turn which is equivalent to four quarter-turns which is equivalent to two half-turns. If they can describe the diagrams with this level of depth they are showing depth of mastery in terms of sizes of angles for Year 3.

Statistics

Pictograms and bar charts

Challenge 1:

Favourite fruit	Number of people
Apples	◯◯◯◯◯◯
Bananas	◯◯◯◯◖
Strawberries	◯◯◯◯◯◯◯◯◖
Cherries	◯◯◯◯◯◯◯◯◯◯◯
Oranges	◯◯◯◯◯◯◖
Blueberries	◯◯◯

Key: each circle represents 4 people voting for that kind of fruit.

This pictogram is about favourite fruits sold in the shop near me. I don't understand why they have half a person voting for bananas, strawberries and oranges.

Can you explain the pictogram to Fahmida? Explain your reasoning on paper.

Use the information from the pictogram to write 10 statements. Include some that involve addition and subtraction.

Challenge 2: Present the information about the fruit in Challenge 1 in a bar chart. Now add the favourite fruits of the pupils in your class. Write 10 questions from your bar chart to ask a friend.

Pictograms, bar charts and tables

Challenge 3: This table shows the favourite animals of the pupils in a school.

Animal	Number of votes
Zebra	24
Monkey	36
Elephant	50
Lion	32
Giraffe	38
Warthog	12

Present this information as a pictogram. Each symbol should represent 8 pupils.

Use the information from your pictogram to write 10 statements. Include some that involve addition and subtraction.

Challenge 4: Present the information about the animals in Challenge 3 as a bar chart.

Write 10 questions from your bar chart to ask a friend. The questions should involve addition and subtraction.

National Curriculum objectives, Year 3, Statistics

- *interpret and present data in bar charts, pictograms and tables*
- *solve one-step and two-step problems (for example, 'How many more?' and 'How many fewer?') using information presented in scaled bar charts, pictograms and tables*

Challenge 1 Answer

Each symbol represents four people, so half a symbol represents two people.

Assessment

Before the pupils carry out the task, ask them to explain what a pictogram is. Expect them to be able to tell you that it is a way of presenting data that uses symbols to represent how many people chose a particular thing. Can they tell you that a symbol is used to show a certain number? During the task, ask the pupils why it is not possible that half a person voted for bananas, strawberries and oranges. Expect them to be able to tell you that Fahmida hasn't looked at the key to find out how many people each symbol is worth.

Expect the pupils to write how many people voted for each fruit, and then to add and subtract pieces of information, so being able to make up statements such as '42 people voted for apples and bananas', '36 more people voted for cherries than blueberries'. Can they work out how many people in all were surveyed?

Note

Pictograms are a great way to support the recall of multiplication facts. If your class is focusing on a particular set of facts, display pictograms with symbols representing the facts you want them to learn; for example if you want them to practise their multiplication and division facts for 8, then use a symbol representing 8 people. Have discussions about these symbols, asking, for example, how many people 7 of such symbols would represent.

Challenge 2 Answer

Expect the pupils to make a bar chart with the vertical axis going up in steps of 4, and the bars to replicate the symbols in the pictogram.

Assessment

Before the pupils carry out the task, ask them to explain what a bar chart is. Expect them to be able to tell you that it is a way of presenting data that uses bars to represent how many people chose a particular thing.

Can they tell you that the labels of the divisions on the vertical axis (or y axis) will inform them what each division is worth? Are they aware that bar charts can be horizontal as well as vertical? If horizontal, the divisions will be along the x axis.

Do they know the terms 'x axis' and 'y axis'? Observe them as they draw their bar chart. Do they make a replication of the information from the pictogram using divisions that go up in fours? What do they do for the half-symbols? They should mark the bar halfway between divisions.

For them to add the favourite fruits of the class, you will need to conduct a poll and either put the numbers of votes on the board or get the pupils to note them down using a tally.

For their questions to a friend, encourage them to use addition and subtraction; for example, 'How many people voted for cherries and strawberries?', 'How many more people voted for oranges than blueberries?'. If they can do all this, they are working at a depth of understanding in relation to this aspect of statistics.

Note

Bar charts are a great way to support the recall of division facts. If your class is focusing on a particular set of multiplication and corresponding division facts, display appropriate bar charts with divisions representing the facts you want them to learn. For example, relating to 8, look at the division of 56 and ask which division that is – without the pupils counting, but using the fact that $56 \div 8 = 7$.

National Curriculum objectives, Year 3, Statistics

- *interpret and present data in bar charts, pictograms and tables*
- *solve one-step and two-step problems (for example, 'How many more?' and 'How many fewer?') using information presented in scaled bar charts, pictograms and tables*

Challenge 3 Answer

Expect the pupils to draw a pictogram with symbols representing 8.

Assessment

Observe the pupils as they carry out the task. Do they reason that they need to divide the number of animals by 8 to find out how many symbols are needed?

What about the numbers that when divided leave a remainder? If there is 4 left, as with the monkeys, can they reason that because this is half of 8, half a symbol is needed? What about if there is 2 left, as with the elephants; do they know that 2 is one-quarter of 8 and draw a quarter of a symbol? If there is 6 left over, as for the giraffe, do they reason that this is three-quarters of 8 and so a three-quarter symbol is needed?

Assess the quality of their statements. Do they all involve addition and subtraction, and not simply state that 24 pupils voted for zebras? Look out for statements such as '60 pupils voted for zebras and monkeys', '18 more pupils voted for elephants than lions', '192 pupils took part in the vote'.

Note

Due to the nature of the National Curriculum, it is easy to run out of time when teaching statistics. So it would be a good idea to look at and interpret data presented in pictograms, bar charts and tables as part of addition and subtraction, and multiplication and division. This is a good way to practically apply this concept to number work as practice activities.

Challenge 4 Answer

Expect the pupils to make a bar chart with the vertical axis going up in steps of 8, and the bars to replicate the symbols in the pictogram.

Assessment

Provide squared paper for pupils to use for their bar chart. Observe the pupils as they draw it. Do they make a replication of the information from the pictogram using divisions that go up in 8s? That is what you should expect.

What do they do for the quarter, half and three-quarter symbols? Have they considered how many squares to place between the divisions? Two would be sensible, then they can mark the half in the middle, the quarter between a main division and the half, and three-quarters between the half and the next main division.

Encourage them to make up questions that involve addition and subtraction, for example, 'How many pupils voted for giraffes and warthogs?', 'How many more pupils voted for elephants than warthogs?'. If they can do all this, they are working at a depth of understanding in relation to this aspect of statistics.

Note

See note for Challenge 3.